REAL LIFE,
REAL
MIRACLES

Books by James L. Garlow and Keith Wall

FROM BETHANY HOUSE PUBLISHERS
Heaven and the Afterlife
Encountering Heaven and the Afterlife
Miracles Are for Real
Real Life, Real Miracles

REAL LIFE, REAL MIRACLES

TRUE STORIES THAT WILL HELP YOU BELIEVE

JAMES L. GARLOW

AND

KEITH WALL

BETHANY HOUSE PUBLISHERS
a division of Baker Publishing Group
Minneapolis, Minnesota

© 2012 by James L. Garlow and Keith Wall

Published by Bethany House Publishers
11400 Hampshire Avenue South
Bloomington, Minnesota 55438
www.bethanyhouse.com

Bethany House Publishers is a division of
Baker Publishing Group, Grand Rapids, Michigan

Printed in the United States of America

Library of Congress Cataloging-in-Publication Data
Garlow, James L.
  Real life, real miracles : true stories that will help you believe / James L. Garlow and Keith Wall.
    p. cm.
  Summary: "True stories of miraculous encounters that offer glimpses of God's continuous activity in our world"—Provided by publisher.
  ISBN 978-0-7642-1074-7 (pbk. : alk. paper)
  1. Miracles. I. Wall, Keith A. II. Title.
BT97.3.G375 2012
231.7′3—dc23   2012028888

Two of the stories in this book, "Tonight I'm Going to Take You to Heaven" and "The Scars to Prove It," are taken from James L. Garlow and Keith Wall, *Encountering Heaven and the Afterlife,* Bethany House Publishers, a division of Baker Publishing Group, 2010, and used by permission.

For more about Jason Black, featured in chapter 16, go to www.jasonblacklive.com.

For more about Willie Beeson, featured in chapter 20, go to www.impossiblemiracle.com.

Unless otherwise noted, Scripture quotations are from the Holy Bible, New International Version®. NIV®. Copyright © 1973, 1978, 1984, 2011 by Biblica, Inc.™ Used by permission of Zondervan. All rights reserved worldwide. www.zondervan.com

Scripture quotations marked KJV are from the King James Version of the Bible.

Scripture quotations marked NASB are from the New American Standard Bible®, copyright © 1960, 1962, 1963, 1968, 1971, 1972, 1973, 1975, 1977, 1995 by The Lockman Foundation. Used by permission. Scripture quotations are from the New King James Version. Copyright © 1982 by Thomas Nelson, Inc. Used by permission. All rights reserved.

Scripture quotations marked NKJV are from the New King James Version. Copyright © 1982 by Thomas Nelson, Inc. Used by permission. All rights reserved.

In a few cases, names and small details have been changed to protect the identity of people involved. Any resemblance to a specific real person the reader may know is purely coincidental.

Cover design by Gearbox

12 13 14 15 16 17 18   7 6 5 4 3 2 1

This book is dedicated to the countless persons across the nation and beyond who have prayed so faithfully and for so long for our family to experience the type of miracles recounted in this book. Thank you.

—Jim Garlow

❋

I dedicate this book to Mary Wall, whose commitment to humbly serving others has inspired hope, instilled courage, and, very likely, facilitated miracles in the lives of many.

—Keith Wall

CONTENTS

Contents

Contents

PROLOGUE

Miracles: God's Personal Love Letters

Imagine you've fallen on hard times. You've been laid off from a good job, and for the first time in years it's uncertain how your bills will get paid. At the kitchen table, buried under statements and notices, numbing despair begins to take hold. Several payments must go out today to cover this month if you're to avoid a deeper hole of late fees, increased rates, and compounding interest. You've done the math, and the figure keeps knocking the wind out of you.

In recent weeks your initial determination to pray and hope for the best has steadily lost ground to doubt and a growing sense of isolated loneliness.

You stand up and walk to the mailbox, knowing it probably contains more bad news, additional evidence of your perilous predicament. It's a beautiful day, but to you the world looks dull and gray, matching how you feel. Your whispered prayer is earnest and simple: *Please help.*

At first glance, today's post looks like the usual: ads and invoices. Then beneath it all, you notice a handwritten, personally addressed envelope. The return address is from a treasured friend who moved away years ago. Contact has grown sporadic over time but is always a pleasant surprise.

She could know nothing of your present circumstance, yet the mere sight of the letter lifts your spirits. The note inside reads, "I've been thinking of you. I recently received an unexpected bonus at work. I don't know why, but I felt compelled to send it to you. With love . . ."

A check falls from the last fold. It's enough to cover your need to the penny.

Suddenly the sky grows brighter. Your heart feels lighter than it has in a long time. *Wonderful!* It's a *miracle!* Just when the constricting circle around your life couldn't seem any tighter, God arrives with reinforcements and relief. A smile breaks across your weary face. Then laughter wells up, a bubbling spring of thanksgiving.

Wonderful. Smile. Laughter. Miracle.

It is no accident that these words go together so naturally. The English word *miracle* originates in the Latin *mirus*, meaning "wonderful," and the Greek *meidan*, meaning "to smile and laugh." *The Encarta Webster's College Dictionary* (2nd edition) dryly defines a miracle as "an event that appears to be contrary to the laws of nature and is regarded as an act of God."

Oh, but as anyone who's ever experienced one firsthand will tell you—and as the stories in these pages testify—a miracle is far, far more than that. A miracle is nothing less than receiving a personal love letter from God, an unmistakable reminder that we are neither alone nor abandoned. We are sought-after children, treasured and valued beyond measure.

In the theoretical scenario above—all too real for many of us—was the miracle in the money (spent and gone as soon as it came)? Or was it in the knowledge of being loved and provided for—a forever gift that adds to your reservoir of faith for the next hardship? We think the answer is obvious.

Again and again Scripture reminds us that God transcends nature's laws and the physical world's limitations. Over and over we're reassured that he loves us each individually and always wants what is best for us. Whether or not we recognize his presence, he regularly intervenes in our lives. Amid our daily heartaches and hardships, we can cling to assurances like these:

- "Ah, Sovereign Lord, you have made the heavens and the earth by your great power and outstretched arm. Nothing is too hard for you" (Jeremiah 32:17).

- "With man this is impossible, but with God all things are possible" (Matthew 19:26).

- "Very truly I tell you, whoever believes in me will do the works I have been doing, and they will do even greater things than these, because I am going to the Father" (John 14:12).

- "Now to him who is able to do immeasurably more than all we ask or imagine, according to his power that is at work within us, to him be glory" (Ephesians 3:20–21).

As you read the amazing and extraordinary stories that follow, never forget who sent them, and take to heart the message emblazoned on every page: God loves *you*, cares for *you*, and provides for *you*—no matter how dire and desperate circumstances may seem.

In *Miracles Are for Real*, our previous book on this topic, we provided in-depth theological perspectives as well as wide-ranging explanations and theories. We went into detail to demonstrate that miracles do indeed still happen and sought to answer questions such as: Is there anything we can do to earn a miracle? Why do miracles happen to some people and not others? Can prayer produce a miracle?

Here, we let stories speak. The accounts that follow are told as accurately and authentically as possible—true stories about real people. No individual featured in these pages claims to have a saintly spiritual life, a hotline to heaven, or a surefire formula that prompted God to intervene. In fact, many told us, "I don't know why God chose to perform a miracle in *my* life . . . I'm just so grateful he did!"

You might see yourself or your circumstances echoed in some of these stories. Possibly you or a loved one is facing a health crisis, job loss, desperate family troubles, or another heartbreaking hardship. May you find courage in how ordinary people have experienced God's extraordinary provision when they've needed it most. And may you wait with confident expectation that God will soon send you too a personal love letter.

1

"You're in for
the Ride of Your Life"

*On United Flight 811, an extraordinary message
saved Shari Peterson in more ways than one.*

On February 23, 1989, Shari Peterson was among the
last to board United Flight 811 from Honolulu to
Sydney. It was nearly 1:00 AM when she walked the
gangway to the aging Boeing 747 for the final leg of a journey
begun many hours earlier in Denver. *Only five thousand miles
to go,* she thought wearily.

There was at least one thing to be thankful for, one perk
of being a travel agent and tour guide: Her new last-minute
seat assignment was an upgrade to business class.

Inside, she handed the flight attendant her boarding pass—
"9F" was handwritten at the top—and the woman pointed
the way to her seat. *Just a few more steps to a good night's
sleep.* The pills in her bag would guarantee it.

But 9F was already occupied.

"I showed the man sitting there my boarding pass, to try and figure out which of us was in the wrong place," she recalled. "But he made it absolutely clear he had no intention of moving. The flight attendant could see what was happening and told me to sit anywhere, because it was past time for departure."

Seat 13F was empty. Shari took it and settled in as the plane taxied to the runway. She closed her eyes and sighed heavily, looking forward to the oblivion of sleep. The truth was there was more on her mind than the stress of a long travel day or the demanding schedule awaiting her in Australia, where she was expected to "babysit" three hundred business executives at a convention. Her personal life was a mess, and the reason was no mystery: She was married to a psychologically and emotionally abusive man, who took every opportunity to tell her she was a worthless embarrassment. The relationship grew more intolerable by the day, but she could not see a way out.

"To be honest, I didn't think I deserved to get away from him," she said. "I secretly believed he was right about me. So I started using pills and booze like candy to make it all go away, even if just for a while."

She fastened her seat belt and reached for the sleeping pills to follow her overnight-flight ritual. However, as she shook the tablets into her palm, an insistent thought crossed her mind:

Don't do that. You might need your wits about you in case of emergency.

Shari stopped. It wasn't the sort of thing she ever told herself.

What emergency? she thought. *Flying is perfectly safe these days. The aircraft are carefully maintained, and the crews are*

16

well trained. There's no reason to lose sleep worrying about something that'll probably never happen.

Even so, uncharacteristically, she put the pills away.

"People with substance-abuse problems are 'para-suicidal'," she noted. "It's a fancy way of saying we're trying to kill ourselves, just very discreetly. So I should have been thinking, *I don't care if we crash and I'm drugged. Bring it on.* But for some reason I chose to follow that nudging to stay alert."

The captain announced clearance for takeoff and advised that passengers should expect the Fasten Seat Belt sign to stay on a bit longer than usual while he navigated around an off-shore thunderstorm during ascent. Otherwise, he predicted, they should enjoy a smooth, uneventful flight.

Shortly after departure, Shari still felt agitated by her encounter with the man in 9F. She decided to take her mind off that, and everything else, by reading herself to sleep. She reclined her seat, loosened the belt, and had just opened her book when someone spoke directly in her ear, as if leaning down behind her right shoulder.

"Tighten your seat belt," said a young man's voice, calm but firm. *"You're in for the ride of your life."*

"I had the impression the voice belonged to a young male flight attendant," she said. "But I knew very well that was not the sort of thing they would say. When I put my book down and turned to ask him what the heck he was talking about, no one was there.

"I looked into the galley behind my seat. The only person I saw was the female attendant who'd told me to sit wherever I could. The hairs on my neck stood up. I knew something way out of the ordinary had just happened and that I should listen."

She straightened her chair, tightened the belt, and tucked her thumbs under the strap. Her heart pounding, she glanced across the aisle on her right and saw the moon, big and beautiful, framed in the window. The plane climbed smoothly. "The ride of her life" seemed unlikely. She'd wait and see.

She didn't have to wait long.

No more than a minute later, an explosion rocked the aircraft.

"I heard a loud sound, a kind of grind and bump, and then—*POW!*—the whole side of the plane ahead of me on my right just disappeared, in the blink of an eye. I closed my eyes and thought, *This can't be happening!* When I opened them again I could see the engines on fire outside."

A fierce wind slammed into Shari like an arctic gale, whipping her hair and stinging her eyes. Darkness filled the cabin as the lights went out, but she could see flying debris as dislodged ceiling tiles, carry-on luggage, books, cups, and more were sucked through the twenty-foot-wide hole in the fuselage. Exposed wires sparked overhead. Even over the thunderous roar of wind and engines, which were only a few feet away, Shari heard shrieks of terror all around.

"I looked down through where part of the floor used to be and saw moonlit clouds miles below. A beautiful sight, but immediately I thought, *This isn't going to end well.*"

Investigators later learned that the latch on the forward cargo door had failed, leading to rapid, uncontrolled decompression and to the structural failure of the fuselage. Along each side of the cabin were two seats in each row, one on the aisle and one by the window. The eight people seated there in rows 9 through 12 were hurtled out of the aircraft in an instant. Only one passenger across the aisle, in the plane's middle section, also was ejected. He had been seated in 9F.

Shari looked left and saw a man and a woman with their young daughter, their clothes whipping in the wind. They were terrified, clinging to one another, but unharmed. To her right, across the aisle in row 13, a couple was bloodied from flying debris but still there and buckled in. However, their seats canted forward at an alarming angle, and the floor was gone beneath their feet. Seeing their panicked faces, Shari grabbed the man's arm to steady him against falling farther forward.

Behind him, she was horrified to see the flight attendant who'd been in the galley when the explosion happened—she was conscious, but her body was contorted, wedged into a tiny space beneath the tipping seats. If they came loose, nothing would stop her from falling out into the night.

"I reached out and held her arm, just to let her know she wasn't alone," Shari remembered. "And I started praying, desperately crying out for help. Then in my mind I saw a giant hand swoop down out of the sky under the plane, and I knew we were going to be okay.

"My mind was screaming that this was impossible. I'd flown enough to know we had little chance of a safe landing. But I held to that image."

In the cockpit, Captain David Cronin had thrown out the book on how to respond . . . because there *was* no book for this crisis. His instincts took over, the fruit of many years' experience as a military fighter pilot and glider pilot. He immediately compensated manually for the lost starboard engines. He began dumping fuel to minimize the risk of fire should they manage to return to Oahu for an emergency landing.

Unable to contact the flight attendants, he sent his engineer below to assess the situation. The man soon returned, visibly shaken by the extent of the damage. Given the plane's weakened structure, the crew decided to maintain airspeed of 250 knots, barely above the 240-knot stall speed.

Cronin managed to turn the plane around and set a course for the airport. He held the craft higher than the gradual glide normally used on approach, knowing he'd never regain any lost altitude. He'd have to drop swiftly, as if landing on the deck of an aircraft carrier.

Shari watched through the floor as they turned around. As she saw the approaching lights of Honolulu, she was amazed the battered 747 hadn't already broken into pieces. She also was astonished at how calm she was.

"I felt this amazing serenity," she said. "I was so detached. I thought, *Huh, so this is how I'm going to die?* It's amazing what goes through your head when that time comes. Things you've done in your life *do* flash in front of you, along with things you'd like to have done."

But it wasn't "that time" yet.

Against all odds, Captain Cronin nursed the plane back, touching down perfectly with an improbable airspeed of less than 200 knots. The landing gear held. The brakes stopped them before runway's end despite the lost engines.

Just fourteen minutes after the explosion, the crew executed a textbook evacuation of all remaining passengers in less than ninety seconds. In subsequent computer simulations, which sought to account for every conceivable variable, investigators never were able to successfully land a 747 with the damage Flight 811 had suffered.

A soft Hawaiian rain began to fall on the tarmac as the stunned and shaken travelers waited for transport to the terminal. Shari looked at the plane, at the wound in its side that had meant swift tragedy for a few, but that should have been fatal for everyone aboard. She trembled as she considered *her* likely fate had seat 9F been empty after all. She marveled that she'd chosen to listen to an unfamiliar inner urging.

In her mind she still saw the divine hand lifting them to safety. And she saw *herself* in a new light—not worthless after all but ready to get her life back on track. That was the first step on her road to freedom and recovery.

Most of all she still heard the voice in her ear: *"Tighten your seat belt. You're in for the ride of your life."*

"I am very humbled when I think about that night," she said. "I've asked myself many times why I was allowed to survive, why it wasn't me in 9F. I don't have an answer to that. I grew up in the Methodist Church and was always fascinated with God. But I wondered, why don't the stories we read about in the Bible ever seem to happen today? It bothered me.

"Now I know: Miracles *do* happen! They happen today just as they have throughout history, and sometimes just as dramatically as in the Bible stories. I've learned to be much more real in my approach to life, relationships, and faith— because you never know when you wake in the morning where you might end up. You've got to be fearless and not so concerned with what people think of you. Be a warrior for your own soul and know you are not alone. God intervenes in our lives—I am living proof."

2

A Long Time Gone

Dr. Sean George had been clinically dead for over an hour.
His wife prayed for a miracle—and a miracle happened.

On the morning of Friday, October 24, 2008, Dr. Sean George had only one thing on his mind: spending a restful weekend with his wife, Sherry, at their home in Kalgoorlie in Western Australia.

Between him and that outcome lay 250 miles of hot and arid coastal plain, rugged country covered in sparse eucalyptus brush and marked by sprawling salt flats and ephemeral lakes. As a rural doctor in an area where fully equipped hospitals are few and far between, Sean frequently worked long hours and logged many miles between distant towns and villages.

But that morning he was more ready than usual for rest. He'd just conducted a taxing clinic in Esperance, a coastal town on the Indian Ocean, only five days after returning from a medical mission to Vanuatu in the Pacific. He'd been part of a team that treated 750 impoverished islanders in four days. The trip had been as exhausting as it was rewarding. When he and a medical intern at the clinic finally headed north on Highway 1, Sean gave a sigh of relief. Four hours and many empty miles later he'd be home.

He had no way of knowing his journey would take nearly two weeks and lead through the cardiac care unit of the Royal Perth Hospital far to the west. He couldn't have known that this time he'd be a patient, not the attending physician. He also didn't know he would die.

———— ⊶⊶⊷ ————

Many times, in clinics and emergency rooms, Sean had listened to others describe the symptoms he began to experience: moderate chest discomfort, slight nausea, feeling unusually hot. But he was thirty-nine, with no known medical problems and no history of heart disease. He simply concluded he'd eaten something that didn't agree with him.

Nonetheless, as the morning wore on his symptoms grew worse, and he could no longer deny the possibility, however improbable, that this was a heart attack. About forty miles from Kalgoorlie, he pulled over and asked the intern to take his pulse. The result indicated nothing out of the ordinary.

"Still, I called my wife, who's also a family physician, and described what I was feeling," Sean recalled. "Her first thought was the same as mine, that I was only thirty-nine, so how could I be having a heart attack? But she advised me to meet her at the emergency room."

Back on the road, his distress level continued to rise, though as yet he hadn't experienced the crushing pain normally associated with a heart attack. Passing through Kambalda, a tiny mining town and the last settlement before Kalgoorlie, he felt an "overwhelming sense" that he must stop for treatment there instead. At 1:25 PM, he entered the town's small clinic. While it was ill-equipped to handle anything but the most routine cases, he knew the physician there and trusted his own intuition to delay no further.

"Dr. Drake was out for lunch when we arrived," Sean said. "I asked the nurse to do an electrocardiogram. When the test was concluded, Dr. Drake still had not returned, so it was up to me to interpret the readings. I was shocked to see that I was indeed having a heart attack. Under my direction, the nurses and the intern commenced treating me with the limited selection of drugs and painkillers on hand."

Sean had time to call the medical director at the hospital in Kalgoorlie and arrange for emergency doctors to be dispatched at once. Then the pain hit. "It felt like having a large person sitting on my chest. And by now I was very freaked out. I couldn't believe this was happening to me."

Dr. Drake arrived and immediately sought to begin calming his colleague. He reassured Sean his age made the probability of a serious attack remote. He recommended another ECG, hoping the results would be encouraging. Sean, now in pain that was beyond the available analgesics' ability to control, was moved to an adjacent room. But the test never started.

At 1:42 he went into cardiac arrest. His heart completely shut down. He stopped breathing and had no pulse. Even by strict medical standards, he died.

In his description, there are two kinds of cardiac arrest: shockable and non-shockable. For the next forty-eight minutes, he remained in the former category. He received thirteen separate defibrillator shocks and more than four thousand chest compressions during CPR as the medical staff, including personnel who arrived from Kalgoorlie, attempted to restart his heart. Then he went into pure "flatline" and for the next twenty minutes received CPR only. At 2:52 doctors made the decision they'd been trying to avoid for the past hour and ten minutes: They abandoned resuscitation efforts and pronounced Sean dead.

"When the blood supply is interrupted to the brain for only three minutes, the cells begin to die," he explained. "After twenty minutes the organ is completely dead. This is why CPR is rarely performed for longer than that. They tried to revive me for over an hour. Had I been treating another person in the same circumstances, I would have stopped life support as well."

———

Sherry arrived only minutes later. Dr. Drake and others told her all that had happened and that they'd done everything in their power to keep Sean alive. As a physician, she knew as well as anyone that the only thing left to do was say good-bye.

Well, almost. Sherry's faith in God inspired her to try one additional endeavor for saving her husband: *fervent prayer.*

On the way to Kambalda, she'd sent an instant message updating her father, himself a committed Christian. He answered: "You go there and pray. God will not let him go."

She entered the room where Sean lay. She took his hand, now lifeless and growing cold. She saw the irrefutable facts of death right before her eyes. But she did as her father had directed. "Lord Jesus," she prayed, "you know that Sean is only thirty-nine. I am only thirty-eight and we have a ten-year-old boy. I need a miracle."

Immediately Sean drew a breath. It was 3:07. He'd been "dead" eighty-five minutes.

By the time Sherry opened her eyes, the room had re-erupted—the still-attached monitors instantly signaled the resumption of his heartbeat. Staff quickly prepped him for transport by ambulance to Kalgoorlie and, from there, as quickly as possible by air to the advanced cardiac facilities in Perth. His pulse was still acutely weak, and he needed help breathing.

Then, agonizingly, severe regional hailstorms that afternoon grounded all available aircraft. Sean didn't reach Perth until 9:30 PM.

There, cardiologists operated to clear an extreme blockage in his right coronary artery, inserting a stent—a piece of tubing that holds open the artery to allow blood to pass—and a "balloon pump" to support the struggling organ. That done, doctors still held out little hope for recovery. Because blood flow had stopped for almost ninety minutes that afternoon, his kidneys had ceased to function *and* he'd suffered liver damage.

"After my procedure, a hospital representative told Sherry there was almost no chance I would survive the next few hours," he recalled. "The level of brain damage I'd suffered was certainly catastrophic. The probability of my regaining any function at all was near zero."

But by that time Sherry had already seen one astonishing, faith-building miracle with her own eyes. She knew God was not through with her husband yet.

"When she said as much to the representative, he grew angry with her," Sean said. "He said, 'You're a doctor! You should know better than that!'"

Sean's condition didn't change on Saturday, and doctors remained openly skeptical of recovery. On Sunday, Sherry received a phone call from an acquaintance in India. The woman, a believer with a reputation for receiving powerful answers to prayer, had learned of Sean's condition. While praying, she had seen a vision in which Sean woke up that very night.

Incredibly, Sean did briefly but unmistakably open his eyes that evening while Sherry sat beside the bed. She told doctors what she had seen, but they discounted it either as meaningless or as her imagination.

Yet on Monday, Sean began spontaneously moving his hands and feet.

On Wednesday, he regained consciousness—and asked to see his latest ECG results. He had *no* discernible loss of brain function. He lacked any memory of the previous five days, but he had none of the fear and anxiety one might anticipate under the circumstances.

"When I woke I felt an extreme sense of peace," he remembered. "It's something I just cannot describe. Words are inadequate. I felt incredibly peaceful and well rested, as if I didn't have a care in the world. It should have been very troubling to wake up in a different environment like that, knowing what had happened. But it wasn't. I've never felt that before or since."

Over the next week, the pace of Sean's recovery was as miraculous as his return from death had been—to the utter astonishment of hospital staff. "There simply is no medical explanation for it," he said. "There's no current scientific model to explain the fact that I was clinically dead for nearly an hour and a half, with no lasting damage to my brain or other organs."

Thirteen days after his heart attack, Sean was released from the hospital. Forty-five days later, he went back to work as a rural physician at Kalgoorlie Hospital, with no lingering physical disability. Since then he's traveled widely throughout

Australia speaking about his experience—and delivering the message he believes God intended him to carry:

"God wants people to know he is still there, very much there. A lot of nasty stuff is happening in the world, but miracles still happen too. God is the same as always. There is nothing special about me. The love he showed to me is available to anyone."

3

VOICE OF LIFE

Kris Sorenson's choice to obey a mysterious command
meant everything to a dying wife and mother.

Kris Sorenson steered his Plymouth Colt into a parking space, grabbed his briefcase, and started the five-hundred-yard walk to his office at San Diego's Balboa Naval Hospital. A budget analyst for the U.S. Navy, he liked to arrive early so he could hit the gym after work. The sun had risen just enough on that warm morning in July 1993 for him to see that the parking lots and walkways around him were deserted. It was 6:00 AM.

As he walked, Kris mentally ran through what he'd do first. There were phone calls to return and a report to file by 10:00. He passed the entrance to the medical center's blood bank, where a sign tacked on the wall invited sign-ups for the National Marrow Donor Program registry. He'd donated blood or plasma a number of times over the years but had never given this program a real thought. Preoccupied as he was, he wouldn't have on this morning either.

A few steps past the entryway, he stopped suddenly, startled by a man's voice. It seemed to come from about thirty feet back, its tone emphatic:

"I want you to sign up for the bone marrow program."

His first reaction was irritation. Who was telling him what to do? Whose *business* was it? He turned around to confront the over-assertive do-gooder.

No one was there.

He squinted and examined the entrance, the walkway, the parking lot. The doors were closed. There were no corners, garbage cans, mailboxes for someone to hide behind. Nothing.

Kris shrugged his shoulders. *I must still be half asleep,* he thought. *One of those waking dreams. Need to get some coffee.*

He turned and headed for the outside stairs that led to his office entrance.

This time the voice from behind was even more insistent: "I would like you to sign up for that bone marrow program!"

Kris whirled. Once again, no one was in sight.

Holy cow! What is going on here?

He stood like a statue for several seconds, watching, listening to the air.

Kris had been raised a Catholic and had strong faith in God, but he wasn't prone to wild visions or angelic visitations. He worked with numbers—with facts that could be added and subtracted, balanced and verified. *This,* though, he couldn't explain with a calculator or spreadsheet.

Continuing on to start his workday, he also couldn't get his encounter with "the voice" out of his head. Within the hour, he was inside the blood bank, signing up for the bone marrow registry.

About four months later, in Toulon, Illinois, a wife and mother of a pregnant daughter faced her own unusual situation. To help make ends meet, Sarah Gibler was working a pair of jobs, including as a caregiver for two people with Alzheimer's. Tired and needing time off, she asked an acquaintance named Carol to fill in one evening at a client's home.

That night Carol had a strange dream. She saw the bedroom door open, and through it walked a balding man wearing suspenders and a white T-shirt with holes in it. With the help of a cane, he walked to the end of the bed and said to Carol, "If Sarah doesn't see another doctor, she's going to die."

The next morning Carol related this unusual vision to Sarah. At the description of the man's appearance, Sarah's eyes got bigger and bigger.

"That's my dad," she whispered. "That's exactly what he looked like." Carol had never met or seen a picture of him. David Rutter, Sarah's father, had died of a heart attack four years earlier.

Sarah didn't feel sick, just exhausted from work, and she quickly forgot about the dream. But a couple days later she nearly collapsed, suddenly unable to see or walk. Her nephew took her to a new-in-town physician who within two weeks had diagnosed a form of myelodysplastic syndrome, once known as pre-leukemia, a disease marked by severe anemia and bone marrow failure.

Average age at diagnosis is sixty-five; Sarah was thirty-five. There was no known cure. Her only chance was an experimental procedure to replace her bone marrow with a suitable match. Without a willing match, she would die.

Tests of family members were negative. Then she discovered that state law prohibited Medicaid from funding a search through the National Marrow Donor Program registry for an unrelated potential donor, which would cost thousands of dollars. Her husband, Jim, was a plumber, and the Giblers didn't have the money to pay for the search. Her prospects were grim.

Yet she wouldn't give up, and she decided to improve her odds. After all, she had a granddaughter on the way and a life to live. She alerted the media and contacted state politicians, including David Leitch of the Illinois General Assembly. Leitch, who'd just recovered from brain cancer, took special interest, and before long the law was changed. Sarah Gibler became the first person to receive state funding to search for an unrelated bone marrow donor.

Kris Sorenson had been told the chances he would be a match were about one in ten thousand and that he might never hear from the program at all. He was shocked when a few months after signing up he received a registered letter saying he was a potential match for an unnamed recipient. Was he willing, it asked, to continue with the process?

Absolutely, he thought, remembering the voice he'd heard in the early morning hours. *This is no accident. It's like God is tapping me on the shoulder because there's something special he wants me to do.*

Against odds of about one hundred thousand to one, more tests confirmed Kris to be a perfect match for—in fact, almost a genetic twin to—the anonymous recipient. One official said, "She really is lucky to find somebody like you. Only a few people ever match up that perfectly."

Though he was a little nervous about the next step, there was no way he'd drop out now. His supervisors enthusiastically

32

supported the NMDP's request that he receive a few days of administrative leave. The program then arranged to fly him to the nation's capital.

On June 9, 1994, Kris found himself on an operating table at Georgetown University Medical Center. He was thirty-seven, the same age as his mom when she'd passed away from lymphatic cancer. He wondered if a bone marrow transplant could have saved her.

A nurse hovered over him for a moment. "It's really great that you are willing to do this," she said.

"I feel privileged," he answered. "How many people are tapped to do something like this for another human being?"

The moment's drama hit him as the anesthesiologist prepared to put him under. He saw another nurse in the corner, wearing goggles, in white sterile gear from head to toe. She held an igloo-shaped cooler, just over a foot tall, for holding the marrow to be extracted. Kris knew an ambulance and a plane stood by to whisk the precious cargo to wherever the recipient awaited.

That same day Sarah Gibler lay on an operating table at University of Iowa Medical Center, scared and fighting for her life. She'd been in the hospital more than three months, enduring chemotherapy and countless blood transfusions. But now her body was giving out. Doctors told Jim that without the marrow transfusion, she likely would die the next day.

She wasn't afraid of dying but of leaving her family behind. *If I die, I know I'll be with God, so that's awesome,* she thought. *But I have to fight to stay alive for my husband, daughter, brothers and sisters, and grandchild.*

So she prayed as Kris Sorenson's bone marrow was delivered, as doctors worked to place it into her body, as family and friends stood by. Everyone had the same question on their mind and in their heart.

Would it work?

—— ⟨⟩ ——

Kris sat in an anteroom in a Red Cross medical facility in Peoria, Illinois. It was July 6, 1995, more than a year after the dramatic procedures at Georgetown and the Iowa Medical Center. He had recovered quickly, and in the ensuing months he'd been allowed to correspond with the woman on the other end of his "gift." Per program policy, her identity had never been revealed to him, since recipients often do not survive the first year.

Yet Sarah Gibler did live. With the help of medication, her body accepted the new marrow—with a few changes. She now had Kris's blood type, brown hair that had turned from straight to wavy, and cravings for caffeine, though she never drank coffee before. Through their correspondence, Kris and Sarah formed a bond, exchanging enough letters to set a program record. They also gave the NMDP representatives an idea: Donor and recipient should meet in person at a press conference celebrating the occasion.

That is how Kris found himself in Peoria, listening to congresspersons and doctors talk about the donor program and the story of Kris's link to Sarah.

Finally, he was invited forward. Network and newspaper cameras captured every move as he walked to the stage during a standing ovation. Amid the dignitaries was Sarah, beaming, her eyes welling with tears. They held each other in a long embrace.

"Thank you," she whispered in his ear. "Thank you. Thank you."

"It was my pleasure," he whispered back. "I'm so happy I was able to do this for you."

Sarah was given back the opportunity to enjoy time with her mother, husband, daughter, and grandchild, which she thought she'd lost. More recently, when Jim was struck by a car and suffered a brain injury, she found herself better equipped to care for him, more patient and empathetic.

Through all the ups and downs, she also has sensed a change in her relationship with God. "Since the transplant, I feel such a close connection to him," she said. "He's shown me just how quickly my life could be gone, and yet he spared me. He had his reasons for allowing me to be inflicted with such a rare disease. Maybe it was to help change that legislation. Or maybe it was to prepare me to better help my husband. It's amazing all that's been thrown at me, but I've been able to get through it by praying and by faith."

Kris, now a Catholic priest, says his encounter with the mysterious voice has profoundly influenced him as well. He still can't explain it but remains deeply thankful that he listened and obeyed when he could've shrugged his shoulders and hurried on with life. He keeps in touch with Sarah and feels part of the family she cherishes. Unquestionably, as the years pass, the enduring memory is of that moment when the two of them met for the first time.

"It was as emotional and thrilling as you can imagine," he recalled. "When I could look into her eyes and see the love, appreciation, and gratitude, that's about as close to heaven on earth as anyone can get."

4

ROADSIDE ASSISTANCE

When Steve Smith fell asleep at the wheel, he woke to a life-saving—and life-changing— realization about guardian angels.

Hypnotic heat shimmered above the pavement of Highway 21 as it wound through a remote and rugged stretch of the Blue Ridge Mountains in northern North Carolina. On this sweltering afternoon in July 1996, Steve Smith knew he ought to pull off and rest.

Driving alone, he was still forty minutes from his home in Mouth of Wilson, a tiny hamlet just over the Virginia border. The temperature outside was well over a hundred, and he struggled to stay awake behind the wheel. He'd been on the road only a couple of hours since saying good-bye to friends after lunch in Pinehurst, a hundred miles to the south. But he had every reason to be tired: The group of men had risen early to play eighteen holes of golf while the morning air was still cool. They'd played the day before too.

Summer was playtime for Steve, and he made the most of it. The rest of the year he was employed as athletic director and basketball coach at Oak Hill Academy, a Baptist prep school nestled in the mountains. The enrollment was small—just 150 kids—but the standards were rigorous, for students *and* faculty.

Above all, his passion for basketball and his commitment to excellence drove him to work hard on the job. And it paid off. Over the years twenty of his "boys" had gone on to play in the NBA. While during these months he conducted camps for youth from all over the region, these still left ample time to enjoy one of an educator's biggest perks: summers off.

It was around 3:00 PM when Steve's 1994 silver Jeep Cherokee climbed a steep grade just south of Roaring Gap. The white-hot sun cast deep shadows in the thick forest of oak, hickory, red maple, and dogwood trees. At the hill's summit lay a scenic overlook he'd driven past hundreds of times, a place tourists often stopped to snap photos of the sweeping landscape below. That day he briefly considered pulling over for a quick nap before the homestretch. The thought of trying to rest in a blazing hot car, with the comfort of his air-conditioned house less than an hour away, persuaded him to press on.

"I can drive all night with no problem, but I always get sleepy in the afternoons," he said. "That day I remember being extra tired. I told myself I should stop, but I didn't. All I could think about was getting home."

He began the descent, the hillside rising to his left and falling steeply on the passenger side to the narrow valley below.

Nine-tenths of a mile past the summit, Steve fell asleep—just as the road curved sharply to his right.

The Jeep crossed the oncoming lane and rode up the steep embankment, then rolled sideways back down and eventually came to a stop upside down in the middle of the road. Steve woke up as soon as the vehicle left the pavement, startled, to the sounds of breaking glass and buckling metal. It happened too fast for him to react or even think.

Dazed, he simply hung on and waited for the world to stop spinning. Once the Jeep came to rest, he unhitched his seat belt and set about trying to open the driver's side door.

"I'd banged my head pretty good and was totally out of it," he recalled. "All I knew was I had to get that door open to get out. It didn't sink in that the roof had collapsed, so there was no way the door was going to open."

Just then he heard a voice speaking to him from the rear of the vehicle. He turned and saw a woman down on all fours on the pavement, looking at him through the shattered back window. Her face wore a concerned but not panicked expression. She told him matter-of-factly to come toward her, saying it was the only way out of the wreckage.

"She was an average-looking woman, about forty years old, with dark, shoulder-length hair," he remembered. "She just calmly told me I had to get out that way. Without any hesitation, that's what I did."

He squeezed through the space between the seat tops hanging above his head and the crushed ceiling now below him, the whole time moving toward the woman's face still framed in the rear window. Arriving at the back, ready to climb out onto the sizzling pavement, he reached for his golf clubs.

"I wasn't thinking very clearly. But I'm a golfer, so right then it seemed pretty important to take my clubs with me, and my duffel bag with my stuff inside. The woman told me to leave them. She said, 'Your car looks like it might be on fire. You need to just get out.'"

Suddenly he could smell smoke. He abandoned the clubs and luggage and crawled out the rest of the way. He stood unsteadily and saw that the Jeep was indeed smoking. He turned toward the spot where she'd been kneeling—to thank her and to suggest they should get a safe distance away. Then he spun around, looking in every direction. His rescuer had vanished like a heat mirage. He was the only person present. The only car on the road was his.

"If you could see the countryside along this stretch, you'd know what I mean when I say there is no way she just walked off into the woods. It's too remote. She was there one minute, as solid as anybody, and then in the time it took for me to crawl the rest of the way out and stand up, she was gone."

Remembering the smoke—and that he was standing in the middle of the highway—Steve hustled away from the wreckage. As he turned to look back at the scene, a thunderous explosion shook the air. The Jeep burst into flames.

He staggered back, scanning again for the woman who had suddenly appeared and just as suddenly vanished. Without her, he'd be trapped inside, struggling to open a jammed-shut door . . . and no doubt engulfed in flames.

"I'm sure I was in shock," he said. "I knew that if it hadn't been for that woman telling me to crawl out the back, I'd have died in the fire."

Before long a pair of cars came upon the accident and stopped. Steve asked them if they had seen the woman. No one had. Somebody called 9-1-1, and soon thereafter state troopers arrived, along with an ambulance.

Steve suffered two fractured vertebrae—the C3 and C4 on opposite sides of his spinal cord—in what usually is a debilitating injury. Upon seeing the X-rays, his family doctor said, "You have a broken neck. It's a miracle you're not paralyzed." Yet after ten weeks in a neck brace, Steve would walk away from his brush with death experiencing only a little numbness in his left arm.

"Years earlier I'd been called on to give a message at the school chapel," he recalled. "The topic was angels and how they're here to protect us and help us. Some of the kids asked me whether I *really* believe angels exist. I said yes, even though I had never seen one. Now I don't have to just believe it—I *know* it.

"I'm only telling what happened that day on the mountain. And I'm sure some people might have their own 'logical' explanation. But as for me, I'm absolutely convinced there are angels protecting us. I probably wouldn't be here today if I hadn't had one protecting me."

5

SECOND LIFE

Stabbed three times with a butcher knife, Bill Purvis should have died. God had another plan.

Bill Purvis wasn't what you'd call a model teenager. Always on the lookout for a new thrill, he'd tried fighting, drinking, and drugs. He'd thrown cherry bombs into a school window near the principal. He'd driven his motorcycle down the school hallway. All of that and more before he turned eighteen.

Yet Bill hadn't done it all.

On April 28, 1974, a Saturday night that had turned into early Sunday morning, he got an idea. He'd been cruising the nearly deserted streets of Columbus, Georgia, in his Camaro with a friend. He'd just spotted a young woman with long black hair wearing a tight blouse, short skirt, and high heels.

Bill turned to his friend. "Danny, you ever been with a prostitute?"

"Nope."

"Me either. Let's try it."

Danny protested, but Bill ignored him. He swung the car around and pulled up beside the woman.

"What are you doing by yourself on a street corner?" he asked.

"I'm looking for a guy," she said.

"Well, you don't have to look anymore."

As they talked, a man walked up from behind some nearby hedges. He was a couple inches short of six feet, unshaven, with unruly hair and breath smelling of alcohol. Bill, surprised by this sudden appearance, momentarily wondered if he was as dangerous as the man he resembled: Lee Harvey Oswald. But he quickly decided that this was "how they do this."

"How much money y'all have?" the man asked.

Bill and Danny had about fifty dollars between them.

"All right," the man said. "That'll do."

The man and the woman got into the backseat and directed Bill to a dark, run-down one-story house in a poor neighborhood. When they stopped in a gravel lot behind it, Bill and the woman—he didn't know her name—got out. They walked to the back door while Danny and the man remained in the car.

The room they entered was small, about eight by ten, and furnished with only a chifforobe and a bed. A feeble glow emanated from a bare bulb in the ceiling. Across the room was another door that led into the rest of the house.

Bill locked the outside door while the woman appeared to lock the second door. He wondered what would happen next. When the woman began taking off her clothes, Bill did the same. She motioned toward the bed, and he sat down. They had been in the room just a few minutes.

Then she flipped off the light. Bill couldn't see a thing.

The floor creaked. The sound didn't seem to come from where the woman had been standing.

Bill quickly stood.

Then he smelled alcohol—close—the very same odor he'd noticed on Lee Harvey's breath.

Something's not right.

The bulb switched back on. Though partially blinded by the sudden flash, Bill saw that Lee Harvey was there, holding a butcher knife nearly a foot long.

The man smiled, and it was nowhere near friendly.

"Now," he said, "you're gonna die."

Before Bill could react, the man thrust the knife at his chest. He winced, felt a hot surge in his body, and looked down. The knife was plunged into him to the hilt. He felt as if he'd been clubbed with a bat.

The woman screamed and kept screaming.

Lee Harvey yanked out the knife and slashed again. The blow drove toward Bill's head but he jerked back. The blade caught him in the neck and severed his jugular vein.

He's a madman! Bill thought. *I've got to fight my way out of here.*

As the blade was wrenched out once again, he punched with his left hand, hitting the man in the upper chest and throat. Lee Harvey started to fall. With his right arm, Bill hooked his leg and pulled. The man's head hit the floor with a loud thud.

Bill seized his chance to rush over the attacker's body, which blocked his way to the outside door.

But Lee Harvey wasn't done. He flailed up and stabbed a third time. The blade sliced into Bill's abdomen.

Somehow he shook off the blow, reached the door, and turned the handle. *I locked it!* Adrenaline pumping, knowing he hadn't a second to spare, he stepped back, lowered his shoulder, and rammed the door flat.

Half running, half stumbling, half dressed, he raced into the night toward the Camaro, where a horrified Danny sat in the driver's seat. Bill lurched against the hood, yelled, "Get out of here!" and tried to keep running. He crossed the street, staggered into a parking lot by a deserted theater, and wrapped his arms around a metal light pole. Then, his strength fading, he slowly slid to the ground, smearing the pole with blood.

Bill stared at the stars, gasping for breath, choking on blood.

There was no doubt about it. He was dying.

Just then, unexpectedly, a sentence entered his mind—he'd heard it two weeks before, at home. He'd answered a knock at the front door and there stood a slim fellow in glasses, maybe seventeen years old. "B-B-Bill," the visitor had stammered, "everything you're looking for can be found in Jesus."

Bill stared at him.

"I gotta go," the boy said. He turned and ran.

Bill hadn't known what to make of it then. Now the very words from that strange encounter returned to him:

"Everything you're looking for can be found in Jesus."

Though he wasn't a churchgoing guy, and though he'd never prayed in his life, Bill decided it was now or never. "God," he said. "Save me. Please forgive me. I'm such a sinner. Help me, God. Please save me."

Danny roared up in the Camaro. Bill managed to get in and hang on for the ride to the Columbus Medical Center, only a block away. He made it to a tall orderly, who had his back to him, and wrapped his arms around the man as he said, "I need some help, buddy."

The orderly grabbed him, lifted him onto a gurney, and rushed him into the ER, leaving a trail of blood. Three doctors immediately came in. One was a renowned cardiac surgeon who happened to have stayed three hours past the end of his shift. Another was a trauma specialist with experience in Vietnam.

One doctor put his hand on Bill's throat. "Get the D.A. up here," he said. "This boy's been stabbed to death. His jugular vein's completely cut. He's not dead yet but he will be soon."

Bill heard the words. He knew his time was almost up.

The assistant district attorney was riding for the first time with a police officer that night and showed up minutes later. After being told the patient was about to die, he asked Bill a few questions about what happened.

A doctor interrupted. "I have to start surgery now." Then the anesthesia kicked in, and Bill was out.

Bill woke up, not sure if he was in heaven or hell.

He was in a bed in a room. Pictures hung on the wall. Policemen were standing outside. Nurses walked by. This didn't look like heaven or hell. It was the hospital. He should be dead, yet he was alive.

Then he remembered. *You prayed and asked God to come into your life and save you.*

He was humbled. He began praying again. *God, thank you for whatever you did that gave me life again. But you don't know what you got last night. You got somebody you can't use or do anything with. If you don't want to listen to me or touch me again, I understand. I won't bother you anymore.*

To his surprise, he again sensed a spiritual voice.

Bill, you just do what I tell you to do. Let me do the rest.

This was good enough for him. In fact, it was the turning point of his "second life." He asked a nurse to read Bible verses to him. Soon he was reading them himself.

———∞∞∞———

Six months later "Lee Harvey" was arrested and charged with aggravated assault. He eventually was sentenced to ten years in prison. His plan, forced on his wife, had been to lure an unsuspecting teen to the house. In the car with Danny, he'd said he was going to walk and have a cigarette. Instead he moved quickly to the front of the house, grabbed the butcher knife in the kitchen, and waited for the signal from his wife. When the light went out, he slipped through the still-unlocked door, intending to murder Bill and steal his money.

The would-be killer didn't count on Bill's prayer and miraculous recovery.

That night of the attack, a doctor told the assistant D.A. that Bill wouldn't make it until morning. Later that day doctors said he was still alive but wouldn't survive. The next morning the D.A. was told the patient might live, but if he did he'd have no mental capacity—he'd been too long without oxygen.

All those predictions were probably accurate according to medical precedent. But they hadn't factored in Bill's spiritual encounter.

The first thrust of the knife had missed his heart by a quarter inch. From a completely severed jugular, most people would bleed out in less than four minutes; he's one of a handful of people in the world who have survived a severed jugular. The blade's third assault had sliced into his liver. And yet, even with also having lost eight pints of blood, he made a complete recovery.

"The only reason I can give you for Bill Purvis's being alive right now is that God had a purpose for him," the D.A. said years later. "He wanted Bill to fulfill that purpose. Even the doctors will tell you that this is one they can chalk up to God, not to anything they did."

———◦◦◦———

Today Bill Purvis is married, has three sons, and is senior pastor of Cascade Hills Church in Columbus, which has grown under his leadership from a core group of thirty-two into a thriving eight-thousand-member congregation.

"My entire life is different from the one I had before I knew God," he said. "I should have died, but he changed me physically and spiritually. God did indeed have a purpose for my life, and I am humbly trying to fulfill it."

He hasn't forgotten where it all started. Every year, on the anniversary of that fateful night, he has returned to the theater lot and the same pole that was a silent witness to his last hopes. He prays and thanks God for that stuttering young man who planted a spiritual seed on his doorstep, for the skill of the doctors and nurses, and most of all for God's gift of new life to a sinful man.

This year, though, he didn't return. Not long ago, a hospital administrator called. It turns out the hospital owned the property where the lot sat. The plan was to demolish the lot for other uses, and knowing Bill's history, the hospital wanted to donate a certain light pole to him.

He knew just what to do with it: install it in the woods on his church's property so that others desperate for God would have a place to gather and pray. Today, if you attend Bill's church, you can wrap your arms around the pole he clung to as he cried out to God to save him.

You could say that pole, like Bill Purvis, has found new meaning in an unexpected chance at a second life.

6

SPEAKING TO THE MOUNTAIN

*After he survived a horrific accident, doctors told
Bruce Van Natta his reprieve from death was
fleeting. But God's power would prevail.*

At the end of three full workdays in November 2006 to repair an 18-wheeler's busted cooling system, Bruce Van Natta was finally confident the problem was solved. A self-employed diesel engine mechanic, he stayed busy working on big trucks and heavy construction equipment in rural Wisconsin.

He loved repairing engines and keeping the powerful machines on the road for a few more miles. While this logging rig had seen better days, all that remained this time around was a little minor reassembly, which the driver, Edwin, easily could do on his own. Among other things, the passenger side front wheel was still off, and the chassis rested on a hydraulic jack.

Bruce began cleaning and putting away his tools. Edwin tapped his shoulder to get his attention over the noise of the Peterbilt's growling engine, idling to verify that the stubborn coolant leak was plugged. The older man asked if Bruce would look at one last thing: A spot on the engine's underside kept collecting oil and dirt, no matter how often it was cleaned.

The early winter sun had already set. Bruce glanced at the clock on the wall: just after 6:00 PM. He looked forward to the bracing fresh air outside, a welcome relief after being cooped up all day in the shop's stuffy garage. The trip home would take about an hour. He'd hoped to be there by dinnertime for once. *But it won't take long to have a look*, he thought.

At the truck's front, he lowered himself onto the waiting creeper, a flat wheeled board used to slide smoothly underneath. He went feet-first under the giant chrome bumper, stopping with his abdomen under the axle.

"That's the lowest point on the truck," he said. "It's shaped like an I-beam, about eight inches tall and six inches wide. There was only an inch or two of clearance above my belly button."

Bruce told Edwin to jump into the cab and check the temperature gauge once more while he inspected. Edwin did—and Bruce immediately knew he'd made a huge mistake. The massive truck swayed ominously. He looked to his left just in time to see the heavy jack topple and then shoot outward from under the chassis.

Six tons of steel crashed down, crushing Bruce's midsection all the way to the concrete floor.

"Blood instantly surged into my mouth," he recalled. "I turned my head to spit it out and saw that, on my left, the axle was an *inch* off the floor. Its top was now even with my chest. I tried to lift it off, but of course I couldn't."

He gasped, "Lord, help me."

It wasn't the first time Bruce had prayed what he calls a "9-1-1 crisis prayer." In fact, in the year leading up to this horrible ordeal he'd gotten the upper hand at last in a bitter personal battle. He was clean and sober after two decades of addiction to drugs and alcohol.

"Becoming a Christian and starting over happens overnight for some people," he said. "But for me it was a long, slow process. Even after I started going to church regularly, I had to fight my way through the need to keep drinking and doing drugs."

Though both his parents claimed to be "believers" when he was a boy, the family rarely attended church or made faith an overt part of their lives. Even so, somehow he'd always known that God is real and available to help when we need him, a belief he'd acted on many times in his troubled life.

"If it hadn't been for God, I would never have overcome my addictions the way I did," he said. "When that truck fell on me, I thought, *If he could set me free from drugs and alcohol, he could free me from anything.*"

After the collapse, Edwin scrambled down from the cab and began to panic. He dropped to his hands and knees, overwhelmed by the grisly scene. Bruce "could see in his eyes" that the man was in danger of going into shock. He told him to call 9-1-1, and with something to do, Edwin seemed to get a grip. The call made, Bruce asked him to turn off the engine—the vibration was causing him pain. Then Edwin retrieved the jack and lifted up the truck again.

"Thankfully he succeeded in getting it off me, yet I could see the jack was under the leaf spring and not the chassis,"

Bruce said. "I was really afraid it would fall again. I begged him to pull me out, but he wouldn't do it. He knew my back had to be broken, and everyone learns not to move someone with a broken back."

Desperate, Bruce reached back over his head, grabbed the chrome bumper, and pulled himself as far as he could. His head was sticking out now, but his legs remained under the truck.

"That's when I died," he said. "Suddenly my spirit was out of my body, hovering in the air up near the ceiling of the garage. I looked down and saw everything happening below. I saw Edwin on his knees by my head. He was crying and stroking my hair and saying he was sorry, that it should have been him. I felt no pain or fear at all—actually, I had the most amazing sense of peace you can imagine, like nothing could bother me ever again. I felt completely detached, unaware that the guy on the floor was me."

Then Bruce noticed something else. Two angels kneeled on either side of his body. Their shoulders were broad and powerful. The way their heads stood high above Edwin's, he thought they must be at least eight feet tall. Waist-length blond hair flowed down their backs. They wore ivory-colored robes of durable-looking material that appeared like "miniature rope knitted together." A soft yellow glow emanated from their bodies.

"The light was powerful, but not painful like looking into the sun," he recalled. "They were very still, each with his hands under the truck, angled inward toward the injured part of my body. The truck was off me, so they weren't holding it up. It looked more like they were holding me together."

Local fire department volunteers began to arrive. With one look at Bruce, his midsection flattened "like a cartoon character," the EMTs felt certain he was already dead or would be shortly. They checked for a pulse. Nothing.

51

Bruce observed that their demeanor was not that of an emergency crew rushing to save someone's life. They mostly left his body alone. He could hear bits of subdued conversation, admissions of being too late, but he still felt detached from the events below, as if watching a movie rather than observing his own death. All the while, the angels remained motionless beside his body.

Then a second group of responders arrived. Among them was Shannon, a young woman with flowing red hair. She moved with purpose and clearly was not ready to give up.

She asked colleagues about the victim, went straight to his side, slapped his face gently, and said, "Bruce Van Natta, open your eyes right now."

When she used his name, he started inching downward from the ceiling, closer to his body. She said his name again. "Suddenly I was back in my body looking up into this woman's face," he recalled.

The pain was instantaneous and overwhelming. Shannon began shouting at him to keep his eyes open. Each time he closed them, Bruce felt the peace return. He had the sensation of rushing "a million miles an hour" through a lighted tunnel. Then he'd hear her voice and open his eyes to blinding pain.

Shannon said, "What do you have to fight for? Because you're on the verge of death and you're going to have to fight."

For the first time since dying, Bruce thought of his wife, Lori, and their four kids.

He looked frantically left and right, searching for the angels he'd seen earlier. They were no longer visible to him, but he knew they were there nonetheless.

He'd been dead nearly forty minutes.

It took another eighty minutes for transport to University of Wisconsin Medical Center in Madison, first by ambulance and then helicopter. Following Shannon's instructions to fight, he remained conscious the entire time. Upon his arrival, the ER staff ordered a CT scan to assess damage to his internal organs. Watching two doctors argue over what they saw in the results, he was irritated that they seemed unable to agree on how to proceed. Later he learned the reason: The images clearly were those of a "dead person."

Major arteries were completely severed in five places in his abdomen, which should have caused him to bleed to death in less than ten minutes. His spleen and pancreas were severely injured. A substantial portion of his small intestine was crushed beyond repair. Miraculously, though two vertebrae were broken, his spine was intact.

Yet not only was he not dead, he was still *conscious*. The doctors, trying to resolve the contradiction before beginning surgery, reasoned that the images must be wrong and started another scan. Entering the machine for the second time, Bruce could feel himself slipping away.

"I blurted, 'If you don't do something *now*, I'm going to die!'" he said. "Their eyes about popped out, but they did take me into surgery right away."

———

There's no medical explanation for how Bruce lived that night. In fact, subsequent medical studies, drawing on cases from trauma centers around the world, show that he is the *only* person ever known to have survived such injuries.

He remained in an induced coma for more than two weeks. His first thought upon waking was to tell Lori about the angels.

In time his spleen and pancreas recovered, a fortunate development considering the extent of the damage, but not unheard of in similar situations. After the accident, Bruce underwent three major surgeries to repair severed arteries and to remove many feet of damaged intestine. Initially it appeared he was left with barely enough small intestine to survive, about three feet (a typical adult averages more than twenty). Then another piece "died" and had to be removed in a fourth operation.

"At that point I was not expected to live," he said. "I was down to 125 pounds and losing weight fast. I just didn't have enough intestine left to get the nutrients I needed out of food. Doctors said it was just a matter of time."

⊸∞⊸

Meanwhile, halfway across the country in New York, another man named Bruce woke two mornings in a row with an unmistakable message from God: Fly to Wisconsin and pray for a man he'd met only once, when the Van Natta family visited mutual friends while on vacation. The first morning he dismissed the urging as fanciful. The second time he got up and made travel arrangements.

"A lot of people had prayed for me," Bruce recalled. "But this man prayed in a way I wasn't used to hearing. First, he asked God to answer *all* the prayers said for me so far. Then he talked directly 'to the mountain,' so to speak, the way Jesus told his disciples to do. With authority, he commanded my small intestine to supernaturally grow in length. Right *now*."

Bruce immediately felt two things. First, a surge of energy passed through the man's hand into his forehead, giving Bruce a tangible shock, like he'd come into contact with an electric fence. The powerful sensation traveled down through his chest into his midsection. Next, he felt a rolling sensation in his abdomen. "It was like a giant snake uncoiling in my stomach," he said.

That was it. He didn't instantly leap from the bed and turn cartwheels down the hospital hall. His overall condition was more or less unchanged. The "other Bruce" went back home.

Bruce admits to being a "Doubting Thomas sort." Despite the effects he felt during the prayer, he had a wait-and-see attitude. But from that moment he inexplicably began to gain weight. His energy level gradually increased. So did his growing suspicion that another miracle was about to unfold.

Three months later, on the eve of a fifth major procedure, doctors had become concerned that his weight gain was a sign of some unforeseen problem—dangerous fluid retention, perhaps. They ordered a series of X-rays of his lower abdomen to try to identify the cause.

The radiologist in charge of the surgery was unfamiliar with his case and had to rely on medical records to evaluate the results. Upon examining the newest film, he plainly was confused, flipping through the file several times. Then he called to consult with the hospital's senior radiologist. The two men huddled in the exam room, and Bruce, hearing bits of conversation, quickly deduced the problem: The latest X-rays didn't match the info in his records.

"I knew right then that God had done a miracle," he said. "They finally turned to me and said they'd gone over everything twice to be sure, but clearly I now had over ten feet of small intestine. Somewhere there had to be a mistake, they said, but they couldn't find it. Several intestinal feet had 'just come out of nowhere.'"

He knew there was no mistake, only God's incomparable healing grace.

Today, Bruce is completely healed except for occasional minor digestion issues, the only physical reminder of the day he was crushed and died. He and Lori are full time with Sweet Bread Ministries, an organization they formed. He travels extensively, telling his story and praying for people in need, "just like that man prayed for me."

"I should have died twice," he said. "But I didn't do anything to deserve what God did for me. It was all about his incredible mercy and grace. And since then we've seen many, many miracles at our meetings. Not everyone gets exactly the answer they pray for, of course. But the biggest miracle of all is when people realize they're not alone and that God will help them endure whatever they're going through."

7

DIAMOND IN THE ROUGH

*After a motorcycle crash nearly claimed her, could Deborah
King find a precious object the wreck had taken?*

"On a beautiful day like this, I'd rather be wearing
sandals than these heavy ol' boots," Deborah complained even as she tugged on one of the boots. "And
my new helmet is so tight. It'll mess up my hair."

Her reticence wasn't really about sandals or hair. Deborah's
husband, Jim, had suggested riding his motorcycle from their
home in Cape Elizabeth, Maine, to Boothbay Harbor for
lunch. Being on the cycle made Deborah nervous, and, indeed,
twenty minutes later as Jim accelerated his Kawasaki Vul-
can onto the construction-riddled Highway 295, she leaned
forward and said into his ear, "I'm scared. Drive carefully."

The highway was in the process of being repaved, and they
found themselves traveling in a lane that had been stripped
down to the gravel in preparation for new asphalt. At that

moment, they passed a sign that read Motorcyclists Use Caution. Almost immediately, the bike began shimmying on loose gravel.

Jim eased toward an adjacent lane that had already been paved, thinking they'd be safer there. The front wheel went smoothly up and over the edge of the newly paved lane. The back tire, however, caught on the ridge. In one horrifying instant, the bike jerked and tipped onto its side.

Deborah was ejected from the bike at fifty miles an hour. As she flew through the air, she saw Jim scrambling on top of the sliding motorcycle as it careened on its side toward an oncoming car.

At that moment, Deborah hit the pavement. She felt her head bounce, twice, before she began to roll. She slid her hands between her legs to protect them as she tumbled across a lane of traffic, then onto a grassy median.

She thought she would never stop rolling. When she finally came to a stop, she heard someone scream, "Don't move!" then felt her head cradled in strong hands. The young man kneeling beside her was an EMT who'd been driving by. He retrieved a neck brace from the backseat of his truck. The next person beside Deborah was Jim. He was alive!

When paramedics arrived, they secured Deborah onto a body board and began to carry her to the ambulance. She raised one bloody, road-rash-damaged hand to her face. That's when she saw her engagement ring. The prongs were splayed and empty, the two-carat diamond missing.

"My diamond! It's gone!"

Jim nodded, but the only thing that mattered at that moment was getting Deb to the hospital.

"Please look for my ring," she said. "You know what it means to me. Please look for it! We'll never find this spot again. It's gotta be close by!"

When Deborah was eighteen, she ran away from home and ended up in Europe. One night, on a dark street in Paris, she found herself in a threatening encounter with a dangerous man and fled, seeking refuge on a train. She didn't care where it was heading as long it was somewhere safe. She ended up in Amsterdam, at a youth hostel run by a Christian ministry. A handsome young man working the front desk assigned her a room for the night.

His name was Jim.

Deborah applied for a job at the hostel and was hired to change bed linens. She attended a Bible study with Jim and, hearing for the first time about a heavenly Father who loved her and had been in tireless pursuit of her heart, she made the decision to become a Christian.

Before long, she and Jim had fallen in love. One day, as they stood on a bridge overlooking the Amstel River, he told her a story about a trio of diamonds that had been in his family for many years.

The three diamonds had been set in a ring purchased by Jim's great-aunt Monic during the Roaring Twenties. She'd lived the good life, frequenting the opera in New York City and spending summers at a second home in Nantucket. She wore an ermine stole, long strands of pearls, and massive diamond brooches. And then there was that ring, with its three huge diamonds weighing in at more than six carats in all.

In 1946, Aunt Monie gave the ring to her nephew, Charles. When he met the woman of his dreams, he took the best of the three diamonds and had it set into an engagement ring for his bride-to-be. They had two sons, John and Jim, each of whom upon their engagement would be given a diamond for their own future brides.

A few weeks later, Jim proposed.

Jim asked his parents to have the diamond set in a ring and mailed to Amsterdam. And when he slipped it onto Deborah's finger, it came to represent hope and heritage, connection and family, and the promise of a new life and enduring love.

After the motorcycle accident, as Deborah's body began to heal, she couldn't stop thinking about the diamond. It had been in Jim's family for nearly 100 years and on her own finger every single day for thirty-two years. Now it seemed hopelessly lost.

She told her husband, "I can't stand the thought of that diamond getting sealed in blacktop, shattered by a steamroller, or embedded in someone's tire."

Jim just held her.

That evening Jim sent an email to members of the Church of the Holy Spirit, where he had served as pastor for twenty years. The next morning a search party of several dozen people—with the help of the Highway Patrol redirecting traffic—combed the highway with rakes. Deborah, at home in bed, prayed fervently that the diamond would be found. It wasn't.

The next week, Deborah's brother suggested looking for the diamond using leaf blowers. Excited, another friend added, "I've got a generator and four Shop-Vacs!" Soon their innovative plan took shape, and a half dozen men convinced the Highway Patrol to again redirect traffic on the busy thoroughfare while they vacuumed the highway, roadside, and median, collecting six heavy trash bags filled with grass, dirt, and debris.

Friends joined Deborah to search through it all. To make the tedious job more fun—and to lift Deborah's spirits—they all wore mining hats. But the diamond was nowhere to be found.

One morning in October a woman who attended their church dropped in to see Deborah. Every winter Chris traveled south to avoid the harsh Maine winters, and she had come to say good-bye until the spring. Before she left, she held Deborah's hand, looked into her eyes, and said, "Deborah, God told me you're going to find that diamond."

Deborah smiled politely. *Chris, she thought, I'm trying to let it go. Don't give me false hope.*

———

On the twenty-ninth day after the accident, Jim talked Deborah into going for a drive. After a month in bed, she was starting to feel depressed, and he knew she needed to get out of the house. She made it to the car with the help of her husband and a cane. In the car, she returned a long-overdue call to her sister. They were chatting when Deborah realized they were about to pass the accident site.

"I've got to go," Deborah told her sister excitedly. "We're about to pass the place where we had the accident, and I want to take a quick look for my diamond."

Jim groaned. How could he have been so insensitive? How could he have forgotten they would pass *here*? The last thing Deborah needed was the emotional and physical strain of hobbling up and down the busy roadside looking in vain for her precious stone.

But Deborah was already getting off the phone.

"Look for something sparkling!" Deborah's sister said cheerfully before hanging up.

Jim pulled to the side of the highway and stopped the car. The car shook as an 18-wheeler rumbled by, too close for comfort. Deborah was beginning to regret her decision.

Jim scanned the roadside. "This isn't the place," he said, pulling back into traffic. He drove another mile or so then pulled over again. Deborah opened her door. Using her cane to stand, she looked around at the endless sea of grass and felt a wave of discouragement. It seemed so hopeless. She was embarrassed that she had asked friends and family—and even total strangers—to come here and search. What a futile mission! She walked slowly twenty feet behind the car, barely looking. What was the point? Was this even the right spot? She didn't know, and Jim wasn't sure either.

She turned back toward the car. Suddenly she saw the numbers "332" spray-painted on the highway. She had seen those numbers on the police report. They must be near the right spot after all.

"Jim, this is the place. I have to look just a few more feet. . . ." Deborah was trying hard not to cry. A cornea infection in one eye made it difficult to see anyway; tears would simply make her vision worse.

Jim said firmly, "Deborah, this is going to upset you. Get back in the car."

Deborah let the tears roll. Her hand on the door handle, she sank to her knees to try to compose herself. She let out a prayer, "Please, God . . ."

Looking down, she saw some trash, a dirty piece of paper, on the grass in front of her. Reaching over, she looked under the paper. Beneath it was a smashed soda can with the word *SPARKLING* legible on its flattened surface. *Look for something sparkling!* Beneath the can was some loose dirt and what appeared to be a pin-sized flake of mica. Deborah picked at the mica, but it didn't move. Brushing more dirt away, she realized whatever it was had some bulk to it.

Picking it up, she held it toward Jim. Deborah couldn't see through her healing eye and tears. "Is this . . . is this my diamond?" she finally managed to ask.

Jim began to laugh and laugh, clapping his hands with delight. "It's your diamond!"

There's a parable in the Bible about a woman who loses a gold coin from her dowry. In those days, without a dowry a woman could not marry. It was their culture's version of an engagement ring, a symbol of promise. The woman in the parable swept the corners of her house looking for that coin. She would not stop looking until she found it.

Deborah had always felt that she was like that lost coin and that God had searched tenaciously for her, just as he does for all of us. He never gives up on us. The parable paints a picture of God's relentless pursuit of us, even when we feel lost.

Today Deborah says her story isn't about a precious gem but about the precious relationship God wants to have with his children. It's about a good God who gives good things to those he loves. And most of all, it's about a God who cares about precious things lost, and longs to show each and every one of us the way back home.

8

"I Want You to Climb the Stairs"

Without supernatural intervention, Bob Henkelman faced a future defined by the ravages of multiple sclerosis.

Lying in shadows, thirty-two-year-old Bob Henkelman blinked his eyes and tried to remember where he was. The answer came in the next instant. It was late afternoon, March 1994. He was in his bedroom in St. Peter, Minnesota. He'd just done something unusual for him: taken a nap.

Bob was exhausted—not surprising, considering he worked seventy hours a week as a car salesman. But that had never slowed him down before. No, it was the headaches. They had started two months earlier and felt as if someone were driving a spike into his forehead. Though he came from a family that didn't go to the doctor unless they were halfway through death's door, earlier that afternoon he'd finally given in to his wife's urging and visited a physician. The prescription: Get some rest.

Now he decided naptime was over. *Time to get up and get on with life.* He started to swing his legs off the bed.

They never made it. His left leg didn't move.

He tried again and realized he couldn't feel a thing—not his leg, his foot, or his toes.

He shouted for his wife. "Pam, I've got a problem!"

Fearing Bob had suffered a stroke, the panicked couple hurried to the emergency room in Mankato, where he endured a battery of tests. That evening a doctor came to his hospital room, a serious expression on his face.

"The tests are still inconclusive at this point," the doctor said. "But based on what we're seeing, my suspicion is you have multiple sclerosis."

A shiver ran through Bob. He had a neighbor with MS, and the man was completely disabled. Bob knew there was no cure.

After the doctor left, Pam stood and moved to the bedside. She took Bob's hand. In a firm tone she said, "I know God can heal this."

The Henkelman family had strong faith, and her assuring words infused Bob with hope. But that hope would be tested in the months to come.

———

Medical staff soon confirmed that Bob had "chronic progressive MS." The neurological disease disrupted signals from his brain to the rest of his body. It was irreversible and would gradually worsen.

Sure enough, a few weeks later he lost feeling in his other leg. As time passed, more body parts broke down. By January 1996, he had no feeling below the waist. He lost dexterity in his hands and had difficulty feeding himself. His head shook persistently and violently. He struggled to maneuver his tongue. Even when he could form words, he labored to communicate the thoughts in his head. He also suffered short-term memory loss—he might have breakfast and then, two hours later, forget he'd eaten.

Bob was put under the care of an internationally renowned expert and his staff. They prescribed seventeen medications, adding up to forty-six pills daily. He also pursued an experimental program that left him with severe flu-like symptoms every other day.

The change in lifestyle was significant and humbling. He'd worked the long hours to be his company's top salesman nearly every month. He'd been blessed with the financial means to provide a very comfortable lifestyle for his wife and three young children. He was active in his church. Now even with a cane he could barely shuffle a few feet without needing to sit down in exhaustion.

His well-constructed life had come crashing down around him.

It was another blow when doctors told Bob and Pam that within the next twelve to eighteen months his condition would deteriorate beyond Pam's ability to care for him. He'd need to enter a nursing home. The Henkelmans reluctantly moved from their home and friends in St. Peter to be closer to extended family in Willmar, Minnesota.

They believed in God's healing power and weren't afraid to ask for it. They went in front of their churches in St. Peter and Willmar dozens of times and asked God to remove the disease in Bob's body. Fellow worshipers and friends prayed with them, often laying hands on him as they called out to God.

Nothing made a difference. Bob continued to decline and became discouraged and disappointed. A few people even told him his lack of faith must be why God didn't heal him. Naturally, this only made him feel worse.

The truth was that he struggled with just about everything, including his faith. Between the drugs, memory loss, regular hospitalizations, and his worsening condition, he battled both pain and depression.

One hospital stay was especially difficult. Across the room was a woman also afflicted with MS. Her hands and arms were contorted and she flailed uncontrollably. That night, she repeatedly cried out in anguish.

God, when are you going to do something? Are you going to do something? Bob prayed. *If not, please take me now. Take me so my kids don't have to watch me deteriorate, so my family can move on.*

It helped that even during the worst of times Pam remained steadfast in believing God would grant a miracle. Perhaps because of her faith, or because the situation seemed so dire, Bob's feelings gradually began to change. Strangely, as his body failed him, he found a new contentment.

I know God is going to heal me, he thought. *It's just a matter of when. And regardless of when it happens, I know I'm going to have a new body in heaven. For me, it's a win-win.*

On November 7, 1996, a cold Thursday night, Pam came home from a women's Bible study with a gleam in her eye. She shared the verse the leader had taught from: "I will restore to you the years that the locust hath eaten" (Joel 2:25 KJV). For her, it was an affirmation that God would act in Bob's life.

Three days later the family attended morning church services. Bob used an electric scooter to get from his car to his seat inside. At the end of the sermon, Pastor Mike Jackson

67

added a pointed message: "Y'all need to come tonight because God is going to do a miracle."

As Pam drove home, Bob looked out the window at snow-blanketed fields, lost in thought. He asked, "Do you think God hasn't healed me because I don't have enough faith?"

She sighed. "I don't know why God hasn't healed you."

"Do you think we should go to church tonight?" This was an unusual question—he rarely went to both morning and evening services. The effort left him so worn out he'd be forced to bed for several days.

But something was stirring. "Pastor Mike said something great is going to happen. Let's go and see."

That Sunday was not a good one for Bob. His head shook as badly as it ever had. His body was telling him it didn't want to go anywhere. Yet that was when the ingrained Henkelman stubbornness kicked in. He'd made up his mind. He was going, no matter what. He wouldn't even bring the scooter.

That night, Bob slowly shuffled with a cane down a side aisle, eventually taking a seat with Pam in the fourth pew from the front. The congregation soon stood and launched into worship—everyone except Bob, who stayed seated to conserve his energy.

After the song, Pastor Mike stepped forward. "I believe God wants to restore tonight what Satan has taken from you," he said.

The message was intended for everyone. The pastor hadn't even looked at Bob when he spoke. Yet somehow Bob knew. The moment Mike finished the sentence, Bob understood that this was his promise, his miracle. In that instant, he was healed.

While the rest of the church began another song, Bob opened his Bible and wrote, "Healed of MS, November 10, 1996."

His thoughts raced. *I got healed. I got* healed! *Wow, God, this is awesome. I can't believe it!*

Then he sensed a voice inside his head: *You need to get up, go down front, and have people pray for you.*

He resisted. *I don't need to go down front. I'm already healed. Why do I need to go down there?*

The voice persisted. *You need to go for prayer.*

Bob stopped arguing. Without another thought, he stood, walked without his cane to the front, and joined a group kneeling at the altar and receiving prayer.

The voice wasn't done with Bob. A few moments later he heard, *Now I want you to stand up, raise your hands above your head with your eyes closed, and praise me.*

Once again, he resisted before finally obeying. After two more songs it dawned on him: He'd been able to stand and keep his balance for several minutes. *Amazing!* He tried to wiggle his toes. *I can feel them!*

Now he was bursting with excitement.

The voice returned. *Bob, I want you to climb the stairs.*

He couldn't help his response. "No way," he said aloud. "That's nuts."

I want you to climb the stairs.

For a third time, Bob submitted. He felt this had to be the Holy Spirit. Yet he also retained a measure of Henkelman stubbornness. *If I'm going up those stairs,* he thought, *I'm running up them three at a time.*

Bob walked nearly 150 feet across the front of the sanctuary and halfway down a side aisle to a stairway that led to a balcony. By this time everyone in the church looked on in astonishment.

He'd been riding the scooter for more than a year. His legs were thin, the muscles atrophied from lack of use. Instinctively he reached for the railing.

No, you don't need to use the railing, the voice said.

Bob yanked his hand back and bounded up the stairs, three steps per stride. When he reached the top, the congregation broke into wild cheers and applause. He was so thrilled that he ran down and back up again.

As unbelievable as it seemed, the MS was completely gone.

———

The next day, Bob still felt like a new man. He sensed the voice telling him to stop taking his prescriptions. He was even more convinced it was the Spirit. This time he didn't argue. He flushed all the MS pills down the toilet and never took another. He suffered no side effects.

Some people had trouble accepting the miracle of God's instantaneous healing. A friend said he would gradually feel better and "after a period of time" be healed. His physician and staff were shocked at the change, but in a newspaper article the doctor described his condition as "in remission." The state of Minnesota required him to submit to a physical every three years and show evidence of being fit to drive a vehicle again.

Bob, however, never looked back. He returned to selling cars before pursuing a call to full-time ministry. He and Pam had two more daughters, even though doctors had said he'd be unable to produce more offspring.

Today, Bob Henkelman is a pastor in Fort Dodge, Iowa. His firsthand encounter with supernatural healing has given him a strong desire to see others healed of their afflictions. In the past twelve years, he's participated in and witnessed hundreds of healings during worship services. For him, the evidence of God's marvelous power in his life and in others' is undeniable.

"I'm just so thankful for what he's done for me," he says. "I went from being a car salesman to being a salesman for God. I'd never want to go back. To watch lives being transformed in this way, the rewards are just incredible."

9

ANGELS ON ALERT

Caleb and Penny Norton bought a house in "the valley of the shadow of death"—and learned to fear no evil.

Caleb and Penny Norton, like many young married couples in their twenties, were idealistic and maybe a bit naïve. What set them apart from their peers was that they *knew* it and had purposely made up their minds to live that way.

When their first big decision together was to buy a house in a poor inner-city Seattle neighborhood, friends and family called them crazy. When late-night gunshots first rang out a block away, Caleb and Penny almost believed it themselves.

Still, Penny had once heard a missionary speak about his lifetime of experience in a remote corner of Africa. He shared story after story of the challenges he'd faced: fire, disease, war, poverty. Yet he concluded the evening with a statement she'd never forgotten: "There is no safer place on earth than the center of God's will."

"When we got married, we decided to make that our motto," Caleb said. "We felt that making a difference right where we lived was what we were meant to do. We just didn't realize how quickly and dramatically our faith in that would be put to the test."

Penny was a high school music teacher who discovered her life's purpose during a college summer exchange trip to Venezuela. She worked as an intern in the barrios with *El Sistema,* the renowned music education program, providing instruments and instruction to the country's poorest children and offering an alternative to drugs and crime in the process. After attending a concert featuring the famed conductor Gustavo Dudamel—once an *El Sistema* participant himself— Penny knew she'd return home and use her love of music to help bring hope to inner-city schoolchildren.

Caleb had recently graduated with a master's degree in sociology from a well-known liberal arts college. Despite the promise of a lucrative career in marketing—applying what he'd learned about human behavior to the task of creating more effective advertising—his heart was drawn to the opposite end of the professional spectrum: social work. He even knew *where* he wanted to implement his plan to change the world one disadvantaged person at a time.

After their wedding, he and Penny had moved to Seattle, his hometown. He'd seen the human cost of poverty and hopelessness with his own eyes, on several community service projects sponsored by his church youth group. To him, the "issues" he hoped to address were not abstract or theoretical—they were *people.* They had homes and children and dreams of a better life. They deserved a shot at peace and prosperity, just like everyone else.

Caleb and Penny believed that "activism" from a safe distance was ineffective at best and arrogant at worst. That's why they made their first home in a tough part of town, where the problems they hoped to help solve would be their problems too.

"People don't need another well-meaning program," Caleb said. "They need good *neighbors* who will roll up their sleeves and do more than just offer advice from the sidelines."

For the first six months, the plan seemed a brilliant success. The Nortons brought cookies door to door, organized potlucks and block parties, helped some of the elderly with fix-it projects, and looked for every opportunity to *be* the change they wanted to see. Their fellow residents responded by letting down their guard a bit.

All that began to change the day Alfonso died. He'd been the eighty-five-year-old next door, the first to welcome them to the neighborhood, tirelessly supporting their various community-building projects.

"We had really grown to love him, even in such a short time," said Penny. "His death created a vacuum in our lives, and in the community, that we knew would be hard to fill again."

Alfonso's children quickly sold the house to a rough-looking forty-something man named Mitch. Caleb and Penny tried to introduce themselves right away, but Mitch made clear he was not interested in getting to know the neighbors—or being known by them. Within days of his arrival, the Nortons knew the "vacuum" had indeed been filled, but not at all as they'd hoped.

First, Mitch covered all his windows with black plastic and installed heavy locks on the doors. Almost overnight, hard-looking people began arriving at all hours. Strange odors hung in the air, filling the Nortons' home with a sickly smell no matter what they did to attempt removing it.

"It was pretty obvious what was going on," Caleb said. "But we were in new territory, trying to decide how to respond. What does it mean to be a good neighbor when you're living next door to a drug dealer? We decided it meant minding our own business for the time being."

That attitude changed one evening a few weeks later when Penny arrived home from work. As she got out of the car, a group of street toughs loitering outside moved toward her, making lewd and threatening comments. She made it safely inside, but that night Caleb said it was time to involve the police. The next day he told detectives what they'd been witnessing and asked them to keep an eye out for potential trouble. He also asked that his identity be kept secret so as not to invite retribution.

Police began patrolling the street more often and on several occasions even stopped Mitch for questioning. They suspected he was operating a meth lab and were trying to gather enough evidence to obtain a search warrant from a judge. Mitch concluded that someone in the neighborhood had snitched on him, and his suspicion soon fell on the "do-gooders" next door. He and his gang began shouting obscenities every time Caleb or Penny came or went. They overturned trash cans, punctured a tire on Caleb's car, spray-painted gang symbols on the sidewalk.

As the police turned up the heat, though, so did Mitch. One day the Nortons returned to find a message painted across the front of their home: "Shut the f— up!"

"That's when we felt we had no choice but to move," Caleb said. "It was a hard decision, because it seemed to go against

75

our reasons for being there in the first place, to make a difference by *not* running away. But I knew it wouldn't be right to wait until things got so bad that one of us got hurt."

That's when the first miracle occurred.

One day, while Caleb and Penny were away, the thugs apparently decided to break in and ransack their belongings, to escalate the conflict and send an unmistakable message. A woman who lived across the alley behind them watched as four young men went to the back door. Unable to kick it open, they picked up the patio umbrella and its sand-filled base and tried to use it as a battering ram.

"The woman later told us they hit the door over and over, but it wouldn't budge," Caleb recalled. "She overheard them saying we must have installed a metal security door on the inside, and they finally gave up. But replacing that door had been on my to-do list since the day we moved in. It was so old and flimsy I expected a strong breeze to knock it down at any time. There is simply no way it stood up to that abuse on its own."

Caleb and Penny were comforted by the thought of angels standing inside with their shoulders to the door, protecting their home from harm.

Miracle number two arrived several weeks later.

Though Mitch had finally been arrested on drug charges, his associates were still at large, and police investigators were trying aggressively to shut down the operation. The area's real estate market was dismal, so the Nortons were still living in their house and had become a bigger target than ever. One night, someone broke a living room window and threw in a lit Molotov cocktail—a gasoline-filled bottle with a cloth fuse—designed to burst into flames when the glass breaks. The aging wooden clapboard should have gone up like a tinderbox within seconds. But the makeshift bomb landed in a heavy iron bucket used for cleaning ash and cinders from the wood-burning stove.

"That bucket had been a gift from one of the neighbors that very day," Penny said. "The fire went out on its own. But we knew then we shouldn't waste any more time getting out of there. We made plans to stay with friends across town until we could find something more permanent."

That's exactly what happened . . . after they received miracle number three.

On their last night at home, Penny stood at the front window—newly repaired after the last assault—when a car turned up the street. She watched it slow as it approached. She saw a man in the backseat lean out the window and point a handgun in her direction. She saw the muzzle flash and heard the bullet strike the metal window frame just inches away. Then she heard the *gunman* cry out in pain only a few yards away, as the car crept by, and saw him reflexively grab his arm, the one holding the gun. The tires suddenly squealed as the vehicle sped off.

"The only explanation we could imagine was that the bullet had ricocheted off the frame and returned to hit him," she said. "I don't know how that could happen—I just know what I saw. God was watching over us, and there seemed to be nothing those guys could do to hurt us."

The last miracle happened just weeks after the Nortons finally moved in with friends: A member of their church bought the house to be used as a rental property. In a lousy real estate market, in an undesirable part of town, they'd been warned it could take many months or even years to sell. But the buyer paid the full asking price without a realtor or the typical fees and commissions. The quick sale of their home seemed like a "bonus miracle," allowing them to start over—in *another* poor section of Seattle. This time they carefully researched their neighbors and installed safety measures before moving in—still idealistic but wiser and more cautious. Slowly Caleb and Penny are seeing their dream come true to create community and serve the needy right where they live.

And they know, without any doubt, that God's angels have their backs.

10

"I Can Hear!"

*For Noelle Abbott, a generational affliction
of silence was vanquished in an instant.*

Noelle Abbott grew up on a farm near the small town of Eldridge, Iowa. Even while enjoying her otherwise carefree childhood, though, Noelle knew what was coming. Her family had been afflicted for generations, and there was nothing she could do about it.

Noelle's mother was virtually deaf. Her grandmother was deaf. Her great-grandfather had been deaf. In fact, while working for a railroad, he'd been killed by a train because he couldn't hear it roaring down the tracks. Because her mother's hearing aids worked so poorly, Noelle and her family mostly had to pass notes to communicate with her.

That silent world awaited Noelle too. She was certain of it.

Sure enough, at the age of twenty, Noelle found herself saying more and more often, "What was that? What did you say?" She had to turn up the volume on her TV and radio. She couldn't understand what was going on at parties because all the sounds jumbled together.

It was a miserable adjustment for this young woman who loved music. After acquiring hearing aids for both ears, she often still couldn't make out what people were trying to tell her. The impairment complicated her interactions with clients in her position as a jobs coach for the disabled. It caused her to miss the poignant exchange of vows at her brother's wedding.

―❈❈❈―

By August 2008, at the age of fifty, Noelle had been hearing impaired for thirty years. Despite the hardships she endured each day, she considered herself blessed: She had loving relationships with her husband and daughter, and her faith in God was a constant source of strength.

When Noelle's friend Sandi invited her to a weeknight "prayer summit" at her church in Ames, she agreed to go. She thought it would be a good chance to pray, revitalize her faith, and see if God would do something amazing for anyone there.

It never occurred to her that something amazing could happen to *her*.

On the Wednesday of the service, Noelle waffled about keeping her commitment to Sandi. *Wouldn't you rather just go to the store and get your grocery shopping out of the way?* she asked herself. Later, she thought, *You don't feel very good. Better stay home tonight.*

By the time Noelle got home from work, she was exhausted. *You're too tired*, she told herself. *You should stay home, go to bed early, and rest up.*

That's when Noelle realized the pattern of her thoughts that day. Was something trying to keep her from going to the service? *If I stay home,* she thought, *I'll miss out on a blessing. I need to be there.*

—⚬⚬⚬—

Noelle, Sandi, and Sandi's family arrived a few minutes late. Hundreds filled the church. The group found the last empty seats in the back row.

The band played worship songs. As Noelle joined in, a strange feeling washed over her. A warm sensation spread throughout her body, and her hands grew hot. Soon, a pastor stood at the front, asking people with specific afflictions to come forward for prayer and healing. Because the band was still playing, however, Noelle couldn't decipher the pastor's words. Her hearing aids amplified every sound, blending them into a cacophony of noise.

So Noelle focused on her own prayers. *Dear God, I pray for total healing from my head to toe. Let me feel your healing touch. I want to be the whole person you want me to be.*

Suddenly, Noelle felt an elbow nudge her in the ribs.

"You need to go up there," Sandi said. "He's calling for the person who has the hearing loss to come up front. He said God told them someone in the congregation has hearing loss."

As the music continued to play, Noelle stood and made her way to the altar, where several church leaders were praying for people on their knees. One pastor looked at Noelle and said, "Do you have hearing loss?"

She nodded.

"You're the one God's been speaking to me about," said Pastor Evan Matheson. "God wants to heal you right now, tonight. Not only your hearing, but your heart also. God wants to make you whole."

The pastor took both of Noelle's hands. "Do you believe God can restore your hearing?"

During all the years of disappointment and frustration, Noelle had never sought healing for her condition. It seemed like the kind of thing that happened to others, if at all. Now, however, she sensed God's powerful presence. Suddenly, anything seemed possible. "Absolutely!" she answered.

Evan put his hands on Noelle's ears and began to pray. With the music playing and others also praying, however, Noelle again couldn't make sense of the noise. She stopped the pastor and removed her hearing aids.

Now she was ready. For the second time, Evan stretched out his hands to Noelle's ears and began praying. She closed her eyes and listened intently. She heard nothing.

Seconds passed.

". . . and Lord, we ask you to heal every part of her ears, from the inner ear out."

Oh! Tears filled Noelle's eyes. Then she began to sob. *I can hear him! I can hear him!*

Evan concluded his prayer, noticed Noelle's tears, and smiled.

"I can hear you!" she said. She thought the pastor looked as excited as she felt.

Evan led Noelle to a quieter corner of the church. He turned his back to her and began to slowly walk away while saying simple words like *door*. She was able to hear and repeat each one.

Next, Evan returned to the front of the church and spoke to the other leaders. The music stopped. Noelle was called to the altar and positioned with her back to the congregation. In the now-silent church, Evan began snapping his fingers.

"Can you hear me?" he asked.

"Yes, I can hear you!" Noelle answered.

They repeated the exchange a few times, the snapping fainter each time, yet clear in Noelle's ears.

Finally, Evan stopped. "Noelle, turn around."

She faced the congregation again and was shocked to see the pastor in the back of the sanctuary, seventy-five feet away. Normally, even with her hearing aids, there was no way she'd have heard him from that distance.

The condition Noelle had lived with for more than thirty years had changed in an instant. She was amazed at the power of God. *Who am I*, she thought, *that he's so mindful of me?*

Only one word could describe what had happened: *miracle*.

———

A couple weeks after the service, Noelle visited her audiologist and told her she'd noted "improvement" in her hearing.

"Oh?" The audiologist arched an eyebrow. "What makes you think you're improving?"

Noelle told her story. The audiologist couldn't hide her skepticism. "Well," she said, "let's do the test."

A few minutes later, Noelle was being hurried out of a sound booth. "I can't believe it!" the audiologist shouted. "You don't need hearing aids. You have perfect hearing. Tell me again how it happened!"

———

The generational "curse" of deafness did not end with Noelle. Her thirty-four-year-old daughter, Mallory, was also severely impaired, wore hearing aids, and often relied on lip reading and written notes. When Noelle related the story of her healing, Mallory's response was direct: "The next time they have one of those prayer summits, I want to go."

The following March, Noelle and Mallory walked into the same Ames church, their emotions a mixture of apprehension, excitement, and hope. Would God bless their family with a second miracle?

It wasn't long before a pastor led everyone in a prayer for healing. Noelle placed her hands on Mallory's head and added her own heartfelt petition. The pastor finished his prayer and said to the congregation, "If you have received a miracle, a healing, I want you to come up front."

Noelle and Mallory looked at each other.

"Well?" Noelle said.

Mallory's eyes were opened wide. "I don't know," she whispered.

"Well," Noelle said, "take your hearing aids out."

Mallory gently removed both hearing aids and then paused a few seconds to listen. Suddenly she gasped and began to cry.

"Oh, I can hear!"

This time both Noelle and Mallory walked to the front to share the good news. The tears flowed as they basked in cheers and applause.

———— ⁂ ————

Today, Noelle continues to work as a jobs coach and enjoys listening to Christian music. There's no more need to pass notes to communicate. Her hearing, and that of her daughter, remains completely normal. The chain of affliction is broken.

"God is so good," Noelle said. "I love telling people my story. God still does signs, wonders, and miracles. We are living proof."

11

A REASON TO LIVE

*After three thwarted suicide attempts, Jamal Dawson
heard God's message of hope loud and clear.*

Jamal Dawson had gone to a lot of trouble to make his
suicide look like an accident. He'd checked and packed
his camping gear carefully, just as he'd have done before
an ordinary hunting trip. He got out his worn topographical
map of the Bitterroot National Forest in Idaho and selected
his destination—a spot he'd hunted many times before, deep
in the remotest part of the mountains.

Unlocking his gun case, Jamal lifted out the only rifle
he would even consider for such a purpose: the Winchester
.30–06 his father had given him on his eighteenth birthday.
He double-checked the engine fluids and tire pressure in his
4x4 Jeep Wagoneer.

The trip into the wilderness had been rougher than usual,
since recent thunderstorms washed out parts of the already
rugged roads. But he arrived in early afternoon and set up

camp: tent, fire ring, cookstove, and provisions. All of it had to give the appearance of normality. Just a hunting trip gone wrong.

Another summer storm was gathering on the flanks of the mountaintop above the camp, and the thin air was unusually still and heavy, as if the world held its breath, waiting for what would happen next.

———∞∞———

Jamal had his reasons for wanting to die. After serving two tours in Iraq as a marine, he suffered from post-traumatic stress disorder, though he didn't know to call it that. He had no name for his intense mood swings and the unpredictable, uncontrollable anger that seized him without warning. Seeming to swing helplessly between rage and depression, he simply thought he was "broken," a failure with no one to blame but himself.

"During that time I was not a pleasant person to be around," he recalled. "I decided it'd be better for everyone if I just took myself out of the picture."

As if the psychological and emotional challenge of dealing with wartime experiences were not enough, Jamal was burdened with two additional traumas that contributed to his sense of hopelessness upon returning to civilian life.

First, while he was still in Iraq, his father had died of a sudden heart attack. He'd become familiar with the pain of losing friends in combat and the devastation of warfare, but news of his father's death was an unexpected blow. Being so far away, he was unable to grieve properly or achieve any sense of closure. His pain and anger turned destructively inward, and going back home only deepened his feelings of loss.

Second, soon after he left the marines, his wife filed for divorce, ending their twelve-year marriage. Her initial reasons were vague, but after some digging, Jamal discovered she'd begun a relationship with a co-worker while he was in Iraq. On top of everything else, he'd lost his family to another man.

Despite all his reasons for killing himself, Jamal had one very powerful motive for ensuring it looked accidental. Crystal. His daughter.

"I loved her more than anything in the world," he said. "But I was hurting so bad that I honestly believed I'd be doing her a favor to kill myself and get out of her life. Even so, I still wasn't willing to leave her with the shame and pain of knowing that's what I'd done. She deserved a chance to grieve and then move on."

His decision made, he updated his military benefits and life insurance policies, naming Crystal sole beneficiary of almost $500,000. She was twelve years old.

Jamal took one last look around his camp. Everything was in place; no reason to delay now. A scrub jay, commonly known as a "camp robber," landed on the Wagoneer's roof and delivered an impassioned speech. He smiled at the ironic timing and told the bird, "It'll all be yours soon." He flipped open his phone and saw what he expected: no service available this far into the mountains. He'd never been able to make or receive calls on previous trips—why should today be different? The thought comforted him somehow, as if the lack of connection was another veil of secrecy protecting him from discovery.

He retrieved his rifle and a cleaning kit from the back of the car. Taking a seat on the camping stool he'd brought, he spread the supplies on the ground near the fire pit he would never use. Leaving nothing to chance, he assembled the cleaning rod and fixed the wire bore brush to the end.

He put a few drops of cleaning solution into the barrel and ran the brush through.

Make it look real, he thought, aware of the sound of his breathing and of his quickening heartbeat. He removed a cartridge from the box and slid it into the chamber. As it had done hundreds of times before, his thumb flipped the safety switch beside the trigger guard.

Jamal took a deep breath and closed his eyes. *Relief,* he thought. *Finally.*

The truth is, that day in the woods wasn't Jamal's first attempt at suicide-made-to-look-accidental. He'd been thwarted twice before by people who, uninvited, had stumbled onto the scene at just the wrong moment.

First, he'd "unintentionally" taken an overdose of pain medication. A plausible scenario, since a back injury several years before had left him in chronic pain. He'd carefully made sure he'd be undisturbed for the evening and then swallowed just enough to do the job without looking deliberate. He would have succeeded had an acquaintance not dropped by unexpectedly and found him unconscious. ER personnel pumped his stomach in the nick of time and later lectured him about the need for caution with such potent pills.

Next he tried carbon monoxide poisoning by tinkering with the decrepit gas stove in his rental house. He lay on the sofa, the TV chirping away in the background, and waited for the permanent sleep he so desperately wanted. Just when the fumes were about to reach an effective concentration, a knock sounded on the front door. It was an old friend Jamal hadn't seen in fifteen years.

"The guy didn't even live in town anymore," he said. "The hotel where he'd planned to stay messed up his reservation.

On a whim he decided to see if he could save money by crashing on my couch for a few days. I still don't know how he found me." Unable to say no to a high school buddy, Jamal invited him in—and surreptitiously repaired the stove. To make matters worse, the man was insufferably upbeat and happy, going on and on about each day being a precious gift from God. A sentiment Jamal chose to ignore.

Having failed two times, he'd learned his lesson. That's why, when making his third—and final—plan, he chose the wilderness. *No one will "drop by" and disturb me there,* he thought.

The sky had grown dark ahead of the rainstorm now making its way across the valley. The tops of the lodgepole pine trees began to bend in the strengthening breeze. Jamal rested the butt of his rifle on the ground between his feet. He imagined U.S. Forest Service investigators examining the scene later and finding no reason to doubt the fiction he'd created. He placed his thumb on the trigger. After all the times he'd run from death with fellow marines in the back alleys of Iraq, now he turned and faced it, lonely and alone. Now—

His phone buzzed and chimed in his pants pocket.

Startled and shaken, he put down the gun and flipped open the phone with fumbling fingers. There on the display was a text message: "I miss you so much! When can I see you? I need your advice about something."

He blinked, unable to believe his eyes. It was from Crystal. He glanced at the signal strength indicator on the phone: full bars.

No way, he thought. *I'm in the middle of nowhere. There's no cell service out here. Impossible.*

Suddenly the past few years of his life came into focus. A flood of questions surged through his mind.

What if Crystal did need him after all?

What if he still had something to offer her?

What if these three "coincidences" preventing his self-caused death were more than that?

What if God really did care if he lived?

At once, the answers seemed blindingly obvious. Of course he meant more to his daughter than military benefits and insurance policies. Of course the most important thing was to *be there* for her as she grew up. Of course this series of near-misses was a message he should heed.

With tears streaming down his face, Jamal saw himself—as if for the very first time—through God's eyes: broken and hurting, but immensely valuable and loved beyond all reason.

He looked at the firearm leaning against his leg and felt overwhelmed by the magnitude of his "almost" mistake. Three times God had stopped him. Three times he was given a new chance to choose life. This time he would listen. This time he would turn from despair and look into the face of hope.

———oxoo———

Jamal packed up and drove home. Eventually, he found a psychiatrist who specialized in treating PTSD and committed himself to a program of therapy and proper medication. The road to recovery he's walked since has not been easy, but after choosing to live he soon found it worth the effort.

He took advantage of his veteran's benefits and went to college. Now he teaches high school English and coaches the football team. Mentoring several students and players has filled him with purpose and passion. Most important, he and Crystal are closer than ever, bonded more tightly than he'd imagined a dad and daughter could be.

"This really isn't a typical happily-ever-after story, not a Hollywood ending," Jamal admitted. "I still have scars that need healing, wounds that may never completely go away. And I still have a lot of unanswered questions about the suffering I've seen. But at least I'm open and willing to have God show me the way. I listen closely to what he has to tell me. I know he helped me stay alive for a reason, and each day I strive to live out that reason."

12

"YHWH ON THE WAY"

When Lorraine Potter thought she'd lost her mom to heart failure, she found renewed hope in an unlikely place.

In the late evening of August 23, 2007, as most people were winding down after a long day, Lorraine Potter still faced several hours of work. Outside her living room window, wind whipped the trees and lightning flashed erratically from a band of summer thunderstorms spread across the Iowa plains.

That turbulence matched her inner mood. She was a schoolteacher, just a few days into a new year at a new job, and already problems were compelling her to question the move. Wearily she resigned herself to a late night.

She had no clue just how long and stormy the night ahead would be.

Around 9:40 the phone rang. Her mother, Emily, was on the line with an unexpected request: Could she get a ride to Mercy Medical Center? Emily, a medical professional, rarely had reason for routine doctor visits, much less an ER visit. But now she was suffering substantial pain in her chest and arms.

Concerned but not yet alarmed, Lorraine packed up her papers—thinking she'd work as she waited—and went to her mother's suburban Cedar Rapids home. From there the drive took twenty minutes, longer than usual thanks to heavy road construction. Along the way, Emily clearly was in extreme pain.

ER personnel immediately conducted preliminary tests for a heart attack. The results were inconclusive, but the staff began prepping for catheterization—wherein dye is injected into the bloodstream to assess the heart's condition and function. After a short wait, Emily was wheeled in for the diagnostic procedure. Lorraine settled in to the waiting room and distracted herself with work.

At 11:00 she heard a chilling announcement over the PA system: "Code blue, cath lab. Code blue, cath lab."

While she knew this was a call for emergency resuscitation, she didn't automatically assume it was meant for her mother. *There are other cath labs here,* she reasoned and tried to focus on her papers. But a few minutes later, she knew she'd been wrong when a doctor sat down beside her.

"He said they had sent the dye into her veins and immediately her heart failed," Lorraine recalled. "She died on the table and was gone for ten minutes while doctors and nurses attempted to revive her. They finally succeeded, but the outlook for her recovery was essentially hopeless. My mom had a torn aorta, and he said there was no possibility of surgery or mending naturally from that level of damage."

Stunned, she felt the world spin around her. Emily would be moved by ambulance to University of Iowa Hospital in nearby

Iowa City. Storms outside had not abated, making helicopter transport inadvisable. The doctor stressed that, though the facility was the best in the state, this move was a formality. There was nothing any hospital could do to repair a burst aorta.

Lorraine's husband, Don, arrived with her father, whose own health issues made it difficult for him to leave the house. They huddled in the ER exam room, where Emily lay unconscious in a tangle of tubes and wires.

"I believed this was the last time I would see her alive," Lorraine said. "I cried and stroked her hair and told her I loved her, even if she might not be able to hear or receive it. The doctors showed us the image of Mom's aorta and veins. He pointed out the tear and the dye we were seeing in the blood flowing out of it. I knew the outcome of the diagnosis was certain death."

By the time of transport, though, dozens in the family's church community had heard of Emily's condition and were asking God to intervene.

Lorraine and Don arrived in Iowa City just a few minutes behind the ambulance. En route, the new reality of life without her mother had begun to sink in. The medical facts made her death a foregone conclusion—a matter of time. For all Lorraine knew, she'd passed away in transit. Her heart was heavy with grief as they stepped from the car and walked toward the ER doors.

Then, crossing the lot, something caught her eye. A shiny black Jeep SUV, parked in a spot reserved for doctors, had a custom license plate that read YHWH. To Lorraine, these letters might as well have been etched in stone, ten feet tall. She knew they symbolize the Hebrew word *Yahweh*, the name for God that frequently appears in the Old Testament.

"The assurance and peace of seeing God's name in that moment were more than I can express," she said. "I knew it was an unusual way for him to speak to me, but there it was, plain as day on a license plate. The Great Physician was there that night. Up to that point, I'd been only grieving the loss of my mom, not thinking of anything else. Just about everything the doctors said inspired fear, but from the moment I saw that name, I wasn't afraid. I knew I wasn't alone and that, whatever happened, there would be peace."

Inside the hospital, she made two discoveries. First, her mother was still alive. Second, doctors were confused by the new imagery they'd ordered upon Emily's arrival. The pictures didn't match the diagnosis of physicians in Cedar Rapids. In plain English: Her aorta was not ruptured.

"*But*," they hastened to add, she wasn't "out of the woods." There was a 90 percent blockage in one artery. They recommended immediate surgery to insert a stent to hold open the vessel and allow blood flow to resume.

Emily was whisked away for the procedure while the family, which now included aunts and uncles, settled in the waiting room for a long night.

Several hours went by. Lorraine managed to get some rest, still enveloped in the miraculous peace she felt when she saw God's name in the parking lot.

Near dawn, the family rushed to stop a doctor in the hallway when they saw him pushing Emily on a gurney.

"He told us they'd gone in for the stent procedure," Lorraine said. "Except there was no blockage after all. He didn't have an explanation, but told us the procedure had not been done."

But wait . . . there was still the issue of brain function, he advised. They were very concerned that Emily had been dead for ten minutes in Cedar Rapids and unconscious for nearly ten hours. She was certain to have suffered brain damage—the question was, how much?

Lorraine was asked to sign release forms for another round of tests. From the room where she was led, she overheard a specialist asking in a loud voice, "Emily, can you hear me?" Then she clapped and continued shouting to try to gauge Emily's responsiveness.

"That was quite disconcerting," Lorraine recalled. "But the doctor said they were trying to judge the extent of impairment even before she woke up."

They didn't have to wait long for an answer. At precisely 11:00 AM, Emily woke and instantly began attempting to communicate.

"She couldn't speak because of the tubes in her mouth and throat," Lorraine said. "So she motioned that she wanted to write a message on paper, even though she was lying flat on her back and couldn't see her hands. We couldn't believe our eyes when we read what she'd written."

No retro-grade or ante-grade amnesia.

Before her 2004 retirement, Emily had been a sought-after speech pathologist and brain-injury specialist. Now that roles were reversed and *she* was in a recovery room bed, awaiting news doctors were certain would be bad, she proved them wrong by diagnosing *herself.*

"All I could think was, *Welcome back, Mom,*" Lorraine said. "And I thought about the miracles we had just witnessed. For twelve hours the doctors had not been able to touch her heart. God did it all."

———⟨∞⟩———

After Emily regained consciousness, hospital instruments still indicated severe heart impairment. In particular, her "ejection fraction," a measure of the blood's movement through the heart, was in the low teens. A typical healthy heart score is between 55 and 70; any patient with her levels should have been clinging to life and exhausted by the simplest movements. Defying medical science, though, Emily returned to mostly normal activity in less than two weeks, while her numbers remained catastrophically low for over a year.

"With an ejection fraction like that, she should have been turning blue from lack of oxygen. But she never looked or acted like a heart patient at all, no matter what the instruments said," Lorraine noted. "She had indeed suffered heart failure. It was enlarged, and she had a little trouble with the treadmill. But other than that she went back to working harder than most people her age, even ones with no history of heart trouble."

Emily has since continued to improve—*and* has continued to confound her doctors at every turn. Lorraine has gained deeper gratitude for each day spent with her mom and for the personal knowledge that the Great Physician, never far away, is always there in times of need.

"I believe that license plate was there just for me," she said. "It was the miracle of comfort I needed to know that everything would be okay at one of the most frightening times of my life."

13

GIGGLING ANGELS—AND A SECOND CHANCE

*Trent Levin's road to recovery and
redemption led through hell.*

When Trent Levin's day began on October 5, 2006, he fully expected his life to change forever. Before noon he would be proved right—he'd never be the same. But not in the way he'd imagined. Not by a long shot.

Trent was first to admit there was little room left in his life for things to get worse. Yet in his mind that's exactly what lay ahead that day.

At eighteen he'd given his life to God. Since then he'd wandered far from that commitment. Now, at forty-three, he was a drug addict and petty criminal with so many minor offenses on his record they'd finally added up to real trouble. He had failed to meet the conditions of his probation by missing drug classes and screenings, skipping meetings, and refusing to pay his fees. That morning he was to appear in court and finally face the consequences—a near-certain sentence of a year in jail in Terra Haute, Indiana.

"I was at the end of my rope," he said. "Nothing I did ever seemed to work out, and spiritually I didn't care if I lived or died. So I'd already made up my mind not to show up that day. I was so addicted that I knew I'd get really sick if they put me in jail, and I didn't want to go through that. I basically decided to say, 'Catch me if you can.'"

Worse still, Trent was homeless. He'd shared a motel room the night before with several others lacking permanent shelter, among them a young mom and her four-year-old daughter. All the other adults were hardcore users.

Around 10:00 AM he loaded his few belongings into the beat-up green Ford Escape he'd been given a few months earlier. His one objective: try to lay his hands on enough money to pay for another night in the motel. There wasn't much time, as they had to clear out by 11:00.

"For months I'd been staying alive by selling whatever metal I could salvage—aluminum cans, copper wiring, and other scraps," he said. "That morning I was going after some heavy-duty wire I'd once seen in an abandoned building. I hoped it would bring in enough cash for another night."

The building had lain empty for years in a defunct industrial park slated for demolition and redevelopment. On the outside it was no more than a concrete hull with boarded windows. Inside, the floors were strewn with the remains of toxic-looking chemical tanks, twisted piping, and broken glass. There were no lights, no running water. Trent had scoured the place before and found a length of heavy copper wire in an underground utility room, at the bottom of a metal ladder.

Back then he didn't have the tools to cut the wire free. Today he "borrowed" a pair of cable cutters from an acquaintance. He also stopped by Home Depot and bought a device for testing electrical current. Twice, he made sure it worked—once before leaving the store and again in a McDonald's bathroom. Both times it made the telltale electronic beep indicating the outlet was "hot."

———⊶⊷———

When Trent arrived, he discovered two more homeless people, a man and a woman, already there. He offered to share the money in exchange for help getting the wire out. They agreed and watched as he descended into the hole.

"It was exactly as I remembered—about two inches thick, looking shiny and new," he said. "I didn't trust it, so I held up the tester. Nothing. No sound at all."

His newfound partners, growing impatient, urged him to get on with it. He braced his feet, grabbed the wire with the cutters, and squeezed with all his strength. Twelve thousand volts arced through his body in a flash of searing blue "lightning."

"Picture what happens when a movie projector comes to a stop," he said. "One second everything's in motion, and then you see individual frames flashing by between moments of darkness—on/off, on/off. That's what happened, as if time itself stopped like a film. Flash, flash—then darkness. I knew right away I was dead. I was instantly flooded with intense sorrow and regret about the life I'd been living. I started screaming, 'Oh no! What a waste!'"

He felt no physical pain. He had the sensation of moving rapidly through a dark tunnel. When he emerged on the other side, he was blinded by brilliant white light, brighter than anything he'd ever seen. He looked down and saw a body on the floor beneath him. At first he didn't recognize it as his own. He remembers thinking, *What is that? Is that a body?* Slowly the realization dawned: He was observing himself. Again he was overwhelmed by feelings of shame, regret, and paralyzing fear over what might happen next.

"We've all seen people 'die' in movies—they get shot and fall to the ground and are just asleep. We think when you die, you go to sleep. That's not how it is. When you die, you wake up. I was more awake and alert than I'd ever been. And excruciatingly aware of all the rotten, evil things I'd done."

As Trent looked at his body below, he suddenly saw two angels bent over the crumpled form. They were relatively small—two or three feet tall—and were made of pure golden light, radiant and gleaming. Though they didn't speak, he knew they were deeply concerned for him.

"They cared for me so much," he said. "They *knew* me. I could feel their love, caring for me and lifting me up. But I was so ashamed and afraid that I started screaming at them to get away and leave me alone. So they did."

Immediately the angels were gone and he was plunged into utter darkness. Terror rose up inside as the weight of his solitude and separation from God came crashing down. The knowledge that his life had come to such a dreadful end was more than he could bear.

"I cried out to God with everything in me," he said. "You have to understand, the words I uttered haven't even been written yet. It wasn't about words. It was about a deep cry to God for help."

Instantly the light returned, and he felt transformed by it. This time it emanated from the other side of a transparent veil. There he again saw the two angels, kneeling before a third angelic being, also made of pure dazzling light. At least seven feet tall, this one wore a flowing robe and held a staff or sword in his hand. He exuded tremendous power and authority. Trent knew the small angels were interceding for *him*, asking for mercy.

"The answer must have been yes, because that scene quickly vanished," he said. "Suddenly the two were very close to me. I was overwhelmed with remorse over how I'd treated them, and I started apologizing. But they were really happy now, *giggling* as they pushed me backward, back into my body."

The projector started up again—flash, flash, then he was back in the flow of time. When he came to, he was out of the hole and "running around in shock." He looked at his arms and saw burned, blackened flesh, like he'd "blown up." All that remained of his sweatshirt was the reinforced collar, now hot and smoldering. He ripped it from his neck and tossed it aside.

He felt no pain. The other two people had been struck by the electrical discharge and were screaming in shock and agony, even though their injuries were comparatively minor. The man said something about calling an ambulance. Trent knew that meant the police would find him.

"I said, 'If you want to live, get in the car.' We ran outside and I got behind the wheel, but the woman had to turn the key because my hands couldn't grip it. I was so ugly and scorched that I couldn't look at my face in the mirror. Even so, it didn't hurt at all."

He drove to a nearby hospital that happened to house a top-notch burn center. His passengers were in such pain and distress that he let them out at the ER door. Then he parked and calmly walked back.

"The triage nurse took one look at me and literally dropped everything she was doing," he recalls. "I was starting to feel some heat in my hands and face, and some swelling, but I wasn't in pain or upset. I answered all their questions and gave them my dad's phone number when they asked if there was someone they should call. I wanted to wait for him, but the doctor told me bluntly that I could easily die. I said, 'No, I'm not going to die. I saw angels.'"

Even so, he was rushed into surgery with less than a 50/50 chance to live.

—⊶⊷—

Three and a half weeks later, Trent Levin woke from a coma. Burns covered 35 percent of his body; he had suffered a pulmonary embolism and a stroke in the area of his optical nerve. He saw a colorful clown and a male nurse wearing a huge blond wig. All the staff wore Halloween costumes.

"It took me a minute to figure out where I was," he recalled. But he knew where he *wasn't*. He wasn't dead. He wasn't alone with his regrets or surrounded by darkness. Against all odds he was alive again in more ways than one. He asked for a Bible and, passionately, purposefully, he began reading about God. His dad came, and a relationship that had been "beyond hope" began to heal.

The miracles kept coming. Upon waking, he experienced persistent double vision. Just before he was to undergo an exam to determine the cause, a man he'd never seen before entered his room. "I'm from Jubilee Church," said the visitor, "and I'm here to pray for your eyes." Trent agreed, and as the prayer was finished his vision returned to normal.

The test found no trace of damage. He never saw the man again.

After forty-eight days in the hospital, he went to live with his sister and recovered faster than the medical staff expected. He also went back to the church where he'd become a believer twenty-five years earlier.

Today some scars remain, but otherwise his health is completely restored.

———∞∞∞———

When the time finally came to take legal responsibility for the wreck Trent's life had become, another miracle occurred: He'd had his court date wrong. He hadn't been slated to appear until October 6—the day *after* his accident—and so hadn't been in contempt of court after all. Hearing his story, the judge gave him a second chance. When he completed all probation requirements, his record was expunged of the offenses.

"But the real miracle," he said, "is that God gave me my life back. I love him so much! He restored my relationships with my dad and my kids. All my addictions were just gone, and I could start over.

"Trust me when I say I really wasn't worth saving. I was despicable, yet God pulled me out of all that garbage anyway. If he did that for me, there is hope for anyone. Every day is a new day."

14

IN THE NICK OF TIME

Erinn Schalm was minutes away from losing his colon
to ulcerative colitis when God gave him a new one.

By the time Erinn Schalm was admitted to the hospital in
Spring Hill, Florida, in September 2011, he was at the
end of his rope with ulcerative colitis. This debilitating condition—which arises when an immune system attacks
tissues in the lower digestive tract—causes ulcers resulting in
persistent bleeding and diarrhea, and tremendous pain. In
Erinn's case—he'd been diagnosed a few months earlier—the
sores, normally limited to the colon, had erupted throughout
his digestive system from esophagus to rectum.

After being sick several months, the twenty-eight-year-
old suffered from malnutrition and had dwindled to a frail
125 pounds. In addition to physical symptoms, he struggled
under the emotional and psychological burden of watching

his youthful lifestyle disappear in daily slow-motion incre-
ments. He couldn't be away from a bathroom more than ten
minutes. Unable to work, he was placed on leave from his
job as a retail merchandiser with Frito-Lay.

"I was in extreme pain all the time and couldn't leave the
house," he said. "I was worried about my future. I didn't
know how long my job would be there or if I'd even be able
to do it anymore. As a single person, I wondered what woman
would ever want to be with me."

There's no cure for ulcerative colitis. Doctors try to control
inflammation until a flare-up enters remission on its own
and to disrupt the abnormal immune system response with
powerful drugs called immunomodulators. Thus far, though,
not only had every treatment attempt failed to improve the
symptoms, it also had made matters much worse. His doctor
held out hope for one more intensive medication course in a
proven procedure that normally brought relief within a few
days. At the same time, he was honest: Erinn's condition was
"as bad as it can get." If the new round failed, it would be
time to consider surgery for complete removal of the colon.

He was admitted to Oak Hill Hospital on a Monday morning. Nurses discovered Wednesday afternoon that sores had
spread to his mouth. His body was rejecting the medication.
Short of surgery, doctors could do nothing more.

———◦∞◦———

That night Erinn spent the last hour of his day as usual:
praying and reading the Bible.

"I was scared, of course," he remembered. "But I wasn't
angry at God or looking for someone to blame. I told him I
didn't know the purpose for all that was happening but that
I was sure there was one. I prayed for my family, because I
knew how hard it was for them to see me like this."

At 10:00 PM he decided to try to sleep. Tomorrow was decision time: Would he choose surgery? On one hand, he knew his body couldn't go on like this. On the other, the thought of spending the rest of his life with a colostomy bag was nearly too much to bear.

He lay back, his mind reeling.

Suddenly the room filled with dazzling light. All walls were replaced by featureless "whiteness." Only Erinn and the bed remained. "It was like in the movie *Bruce Almighty*, when Jim Carrey is 'in heaven' with Morgan Freeman—it looked like a huge, empty white room," he said. "The light was really bright but didn't hurt my eyes. It seemed to come from everywhere at once."

A man's voice spoke Erinn's name. It sounded perfectly ordinary, like it could belong to anyone. He looked left and saw nothing.

The voice called him again. He turned to the right; a "heavenly figure" stood beside the bed. Dressed in a flowing white robe, he was about Erinn's height and build but shrouded in bright light that made his features indistinct.

The being pointed to his left, where another "body" stood that was unlike anything Erinn had ever seen. It was naked, with distinct shape and form, yet was transparent as if made of a sort of "gel." Erinn recognized it immediately. It looked exactly like *him*.

"What do you think?" the being asked.

"Can I try it out?" Erinn responded.

The answer was yes.

Bounding out of bed, Erinn positioned himself beside the heavenly doppelgänger, unsure what to do next. He leaned into it. Instantly the two bodies "merged together."

"I could no longer feel *any* pain," he recalled. "I felt better than ever before, even better than when I wasn't sick. I began to run around, doing anything I could to try wearing out this new body. But no matter what, I didn't even need to breathe. I couldn't feel my heart beating. This new body never got tired or felt any discomfort. Everything it needed seemed to flow effortlessly through it like a river. It was amazing."

Then, without warning, the room returned to normal and he was back in bed. He opened his eyes and looked at the clock: Forty-five minutes had gone by while he frolicked. He cried in gratitude for the miraculous promise conveyed by the vision.

"I didn't know if it meant God had plans to heal me or if he was just letting me glimpse what waited for me at the end of my life when he finally calls my name," Erinn said. "Either way it gave me something better to look forward to, and I knew for sure that heaven is going to be *awesome*."

For the next half hour, he continued to feel no pain of any kind. He didn't even have the usual soreness where numerous intravenous tubes were attached. Gradually the pain returned, and the effortless "flow" he'd felt in his other body gave way to the familiar sensations in his old one. He fell asleep.

By the following Monday, Erinn's condition remained unchanged, and his mind was made up. After consulting with his parents and siblings, he decided to go ahead with surgery—the only medical option left. Other treatments had not worked, and doctors concluded this was unlikely to change. If he regained his life by losing his colon, he thought, that would be a worthwhile bargain. The operation was scheduled for a week later, the following Monday morning.

His gastrologist made one last visit Sunday afternoon. He gently pressed on the young man's abdomen, as he usually did, to gauge the swelling and the amount of tenderness. This time he furrowed his brow and seemed confused by what he felt. He told Erinn his colon was not as "hard" as just a few days earlier; this could signal an unexpected change. To be safe, the man ordered one more round of diagnostic tests, called a "lower GI," prior to surgery.

Erinn's parents arrived early on Monday to spend time comforting and praying with their son.

"They wanted to be sure I was mentally prepared—I was in really bad shape," he said. "We prayed a very emotional prayer and acknowledged that with God anything is possible. He could still heal me, but we asked him, if it was his will for me to have surgery, to bless the hands doing it."

Around 8:00 AM he was given general anesthesia. He would undergo the lower GI for one last look at his colon. If that procedure revealed nothing new, he'd remain unconscious and go straight to surgery.

Sometime later Erinn woke in his now-familiar room . . . and instantly he felt better. He had no pain or discomfort. Initially he chalked it up to lingering effects of anesthesia, or perhaps wishful thinking. In any case, he felt *good* for the first time in months. Then he noticed that no surgery had been done.

His doctor entered, carrying the results of the last-minute colonoscopy.

"Well, I can't believe it," he said. "These pictures show that you are healed. There's not even any scar tissue. It is as if you never had UC at all!"

"I think that's the only time I ever saw my dad cry," he recalled. "We knew God had answered our prayers and done a miracle. The doctor wasn't so sure about that, wanting to credit the medication after all, but it didn't matter. We knew better. We laughed and cried and hugged and gave thanks."

Erinn left that day, over the objections of the doctor who wanted to keep him for further observation. To the amazement of his co-workers, who'd seen him in dire straits just two weeks earlier, he returned to work within days. He's since had countless opportunities to tell concerned friends and acquaintances exactly how God healed him and how the experience has changed the way he looks at life.

"I have a lot more compassion now for people who are sick," he said. "I understand how it feels to nearly lose hope. I wanted to give up so many times, but God got me through it. Then, at the last minute, he rescued me. I learned that he never gives me something I can't handle. And even if things don't happen how or when I want them to, he's always there. He always cares."

Today, Erinn is more active and energetic than at any time since he was a teenager. He remains completely free of all the symptoms that had caused him such pain and distress. Though he's never again experienced the power and freedom of his "heavenly body," he knows it's there waiting for him, one day.

15

"JUMP—GOD WILL CATCH YOU"

*Jerry and Tina Landry's reward for following God
into uncharted territory was manna from heaven.*

Checking the mailbox, often several times a day, had
become a nervous compulsion for Jerry Landry in
late May 2002. Not normally an obsessive sort, he
and his wife, Tina, had made big plans that depended on an
insurance settlement they were owed. The check was already a
month overdue, and a moment of truth was fast approaching.

After serving eight years in the army, he'd been back in civilian life for two years, settling the family in Colorado Springs.
His timing could have been better: The country was still in the
post–9/11 economic slump, and good-paying positions were
hard to come by, even for veterans. With four young kids to
support, they struggled to make ends meet. He was working
two dead-end jobs with little hope of advancement, so they

decided he might as well take advantage of the education benefits he'd accrued and go to college.

It would be tough financially. But perhaps by graduation time the job market would have improved.

And they had another goal in mind: move their family to a smaller town in the mountains. As it was, they spent every spare weekend driving westward over the Rocky Mountains Front Range for camping and hiking. For school, Jerry chose Western State College in Gunnison, a sleepy ranch town at nearly eight thousand feet, just west of the Continental Divide.

"We were ready for a big change," he said. "But it also seemed like a big risk. We'd already made the leap into civilian life after years in the army. Now we were getting ready to do it again. Yet every time we prayed about it, we had a sense of confidence and peace."

———— ∞∞∞ ————

About a year after Jerry left the military, Tina suffered minor injuries in a traffic accident. The other driver was clearly at fault, and his insurance company reluctantly agreed to settle a claim to cover medical expenses plus a little extra. It wasn't a fortune, but it was enough to bankroll the family's move with cushion. Without it they could not have afforded the first- and last-month's rent and security deposit necessary for a new place to live.

Having been assured by the claims agent that payment was approved and on its way, they made final plans to move the first week of June, just six weeks away. They allowed plenty of time to get settled through the summer before fall semester began. Jerry applied to the college and was accepted. He gave notice at work and informed the landlord of their intention not to renew their lease. He applied for new jobs from a distance and had at least one promising lead. The family began saying good-bye to friends. Everything was going according to plan, *except* that a week before moving day the check still had not arrived.

"It was absolutely nerve-racking," Jerry said. "Our apartment had been rented to someone else—we'd crossed a point of no return. We couldn't go forward or backward. Believe me, we were questioning ourselves pretty heavily, and God too, for that matter. Why had he seemed to give us a green light only to put us through this stress?"

With five days to go, something did arrive in the mailbox—a letter saying that payment was delayed pending a final review. Suddenly the check wasn't just late; it wasn't coming at all, at least not in time to be of any use in their current predicament. It was a tight spot from which they saw no escape. One way or another they were days from being homeless, since they lacked the money to sign a new lease no matter where they were.

That evening, with the kids asleep, the couple sat at the kitchen table to try to decide what to do next. The hardest part was feeling they'd been foolish to proceed so decisively without having the resources in hand. It was tempting for Jerry to question his judgment all the way back to leaving the relative security of military life. Yet the conversation always circled back to an undeniable fact: All along they'd consistently felt confident of God's approval.

What could that mean?

"Maybe we should just pack up and go anyway," Tina said. "Maybe what we have is enough, even though it doesn't look like it." She reminded Jerry of the Bible story about the five loaves and two fishes, which Jesus used to feed thousands of people.

He conceded her point—in theory. It certainly would take a miracle to make what they had be enough. He took his role

113

as his kids' provider and protector very seriously and wasn't about to move them to a strange town without a safety net, unless God gave him an unmistakable signal to do so.

He'd just said as much to Tina, when there was a knock at the door. Faye, the mid-sixty-something woman who lived alone in the apartment above, had taken a grandmotherly interest in the Landry children from the day they'd moved in, frequently bringing treats and inviting them for tea. She was a Christian, and though she didn't make a point of openly discussing her faith, it was apparent in the well-worn Bible on the end table by her favorite chair, and more so in the quiet grace that surrounded her like a gentle glow.

The couple invited her in, but Faye said she had only a moment. Standing in the doorway, she handed Tina an envelope bearing their neatly written names. It contained $50 in cash, which she described as her "blessing for their journey." Then she told them she'd been praying about their upcoming move and had received a message from God.

"She was generally aware of our plans, but knew nothing of our present crisis," Jerry recalled. "Her statement about having a message for us took me by surprise, since the subject of God had never come up before. Yet she said it so easily and unapologetically, like it was the most natural thing in the world."

The short message—just five words—packed a powerful punch.

"Jump," she said. "God will catch you."

———⚮———

So they jumped. On Saturday, June 6, the Landry family arrived in Gunnison. The dark spruce and pine forests at higher elevations were tinted with the bright spring-green of new aspen leaves. The sky was deep blue and cloudless.

114

They found a campsite north of town along the Taylor River, swollen with spring snowmelt.

All weekend long they watched rafters and kayakers navigate the rapids. The kids had a blast climbing granite boulders and chasing a gang of thieving gray squirrels back into the towering trees.

"Watching them play was an eye-opener for me," Jerry said. "They didn't have a care in the world, even though our situation still had the potential to end badly. I tried my hardest all weekend to be like them, to just let go and trust that somehow things would work out."

They had made up their minds to simply relax for the weekend, resisting the temptation to rush into town and start pounding the pavement for a job and a place to live. They decided to honor the Sabbath, and demonstrate their trust, by doing nothing at all. And it paid off in momentary peace of mind. The family had more fun together in those two days than they'd had in months.

Then Monday morning arrived, and Jerry woke with an iron ball of fear in his stomach. The sun had risen on another beautiful mountain day, but he could see only the "reality" of just how risky this move had been and what a long shot it was to expect everything to fall into place. He mechanically ate breakfast, sickening dread steadily growing. The children were still immersed in adventurous play, but this time he couldn't follow them. Now he felt the weight of their well-being squarely on his "inadequate" shoulders.

Just as the warm sun was cresting the canyon walls, they loaded the kids into the car and headed to town. Their first stop would be the Job Service Center, a state-run employment office right on Main Street. Jerry had spent hours on the phone with a clerk, exploring a variety of opportunities. One in particular, a seasonal job with the U.S. Forest Service, looked promising.

He parked across the street; Tina and the kids would wait. Inside he'd barely finished introducing himself when the woman said all positions he'd applied for were filled. All she had available at the moment were day labor opportunities. She pointed to the bulletin board where notices were posted.

"The fear I'd been wrestling with all morning suddenly got heavier," he remembered. "I had no idea what to do next. Somehow I managed to say, 'Okay, God, here we are. What are you going to do with us?'"

He turned to leave the office and deliver the bad news. As he reached for the doorknob, the clerk called his name. She was approaching him with what looked like an invoice. Something was handwritten across the back.

"There *is* this opening," she said. "It came up a few minutes before you got here. We haven't even had time to post it yet. I don't know if you'd be interested. It's a full-time position delivering furniture."

Jerry assured her he was most definitely interested. Grasping the paper she offered, he asked who he should contact.

"Go out and turn left," she said. "The first door you come to is the furniture store. Tell them I sent you."

He thanked her and once more headed out the door.

"Oh, and one more thing," she said. "If you don't already have a place to live, the job comes with a house."

Twenty minutes later, the interview finished, and Jerry was no longer unemployed. He crossed the street and got back in the car. The aching dread was replaced by amazement and wonder. He told Tina the details of what God had just done:

With less than half an hour in town he'd found a good job and a house at reduced rent. The place would be ready in a week. Further, his new employers/landlords didn't require first- and last-month's rent or a security deposit. They were as happy to hire him as he was to find work.

"A lot of people have heard this story over the years and said we were so 'lucky' to be in the right place at the right time," Jerry noted. "But we know there was more to it than that. God said if we would trust him he'd take care of us. And he did it in such a way that we couldn't deny it was him. As miracles go, it wasn't as dramatic as some. But it sure touched our lives and taught us something about childlike trust."

Four years later he graduated—and the family has never regretted their adventurous move to the mountains.

16

AFTER THE "GUILLOTINE"

A freak accident destroyed opera singer Jason Black's voice.
But then God turned "permanent" into "temporary."

L ike most everyone who has endured the ordeal of "moving day," Jason Black was tempted to vow he'd never move again. How had he and his wife, Tausha, managed to collect so much stuff in just two years of marriage?

On the bright side, all that remained in the town house they were vacating in Burbank, California, were the heavy appliances and the massive glass tabletop he'd agreed to store for a friend. Fortunately, he'd hired a couple of teenagers from church for the afternoon. The monstrous slab weighed well over a hundred pounds and was awkward to maneuver. It was no wonder he'd left it for last.

The hassle notwithstanding, Jason knew the move was a good thing. His career had just taken a giant leap forward with contracts in hand to perform at the Los Angeles Opera and Orange County Opera. Years of training and hard work were beginning to pay off. After a near-fatal car accident in 1999—and a miraculous recovery against all medical odds— his renewed lease on life had the earmarks of a real Cinderella story. The new house was bigger and had a backyard with plenty of room to accommodate Jaxon, their "dream dog," a 75-pound black lab the couple had always wanted.

One of the boys he'd hired was his own size—six feet tall, 170 pounds. The other, a big-hearted young man, had the build of a linebacker, weighing in at 240 and standing tall at six feet four. Of all the kids in the youth group, he looked most perfect for the job.

Since the tabletop measured about six feet on all sides, they would need to carry it upright, gripping only the edges, which required a lot of hand and upper-body strength. But he was confident the young men could handle it. They'd do the lifting while he spotted them through the doorway to avoid banging it. Tausha was glad to be a spectator and not a participant.

———— ∞ ————

As they inched through the house, the smaller boy lost his grip and dropped one end. When the corner dug into the hardwood floor with a thud, he apologized and quickly assured Jason he could manage.

They lifted the glass again and headed for the door. Then the "linebacker" dropped his end as well, leaving another floor gash.

"At this point we stopped and had a heart-to-heart," Jason recalled. "I asked, 'Are you sure about this?' The big guy said, 'My fault. I can handle it.' But after two drops in a row, I decided I'd better take over on one end. I'd moved it before, so I knew I could do it."

With Jason on one end and the larger boy on the other—space didn't allow for two to share the load on an end—they reached the front door. The younger guy went through first, moving backward and stooping as low as possible so the glass could clear the lintel. Jason leaned over as well, his right shoulder, face, and neck pressing hard against the glass.

Then abruptly the big guy dropped his end again, only this time he stood over the hard concrete doorstep instead of the wood floor.

The tabletop broke in two along a crack that ran above Jason's head. The piece on top was now free to fall. It did, and it sliced across his exposed neck. The razor-sharp edge severed both jugular veins and the nerves leading to his right arm.

He fell to the floor. So did the rest of the glass, though without causing further injury to anyone.

Jason knew the trauma would hit Tausha like a ton of bricks. Only a few years earlier, she and Jason were involved in an accident that pinned him in the vehicle "for what seemed like forever" as the Jaws of Life took twenty minutes to free him from the wreckage. All the while she'd suffered through her own injuries while listening to him cry out in pain.

Still, he yelled, "Call 9-1-1!"

Then Jason told the "linebacker" to hold him upside down to keep what little blood he had left flowing to his brain to keep him conscious. He told the smaller guy to grab a moving blanket to stanch the flow of blood. A neighbor who'd seen the accident rushed over with clean cloth diapers to use instead.

The smaller young man held Jason's neck closed while Tausha called for help. A fire station was around the corner, and an ambulance arrived within minutes. Although conventional wisdom says Jason should have died within minutes, by the grace of God and the quick actions of those around him, he never even lost consciousness.

"When they loaded me in, I decided I'd better pray," he said. "I come from a family of ministers. I figured that saying exactly what Jesus taught us to pray was the best approach, so I started to say the Lord's Prayer. Ordinarily I know it frontward and backward, but that day I couldn't remember a single word. Under the circumstances, I trusted it was enough just to *think* of asking for God's help."

St. Joseph's Medical Center was a mile away. But emergency responders recognized that Jason needed a fully staffed and equipped trauma center, and they determined to transport him through LA traffic to Cedars-Sinai Medical Center in West Hollywood, at least half an hour away.

In the ambulance, Jason experienced pain "beyond description" as the EMT reached into the wound to hold the severed veins together as best he could. Jason's blood loss was so rapid and so severe that he and the medical team could "hear" the blood pumping from his body.

"I felt the most tired I can ever remember being in my life," he recalled. "All I had to do was shut my eyes and I'd fall into the most peaceful, warm, comfortable place ever, and just go to sleep. But I knew if I did, I'd die and not come back. I had to choose: sleep or stay with the pain and fight through it. I spent a lot of energy staying awake."

He knew the ER staff's primary concern was to do everything possible to save his life. Nevertheless, upon arrival he tried to impress upon them also to be careful with his *voice*. He knew from previous experience in emergency surgery that doctors are not always careful about "secondary concerns" when faced with potentially fatal trauma. Still, he'd spent years turning his voice into a finely honed instrument. He was somehow confident he'd survive the operation and wanted to come through it with his career intact as well.

———∞∞∞———

Jason awoke in recovery several hours later, grateful to be alive. No one in the ER could recall someone surviving injuries so severe. But he quickly discovered he was unable to move his right arm, and doctors informed him this was irreversible. The muscles in his right diaphragm were paralyzed as well, restricting his ability to breathe.

What's more, he couldn't speak. He could not even whisper, for his right vocal cord also was paralyzed. Normally speech is possible because the vocal cords come together in the windpipe, opening and closing like two Japanese folding fans. The accident had severed the nerve, freezing the right cord in the open position. Before surgery he'd feared waking with a *damaged* voice. To have no voice at all was a dreadful shock.

"The cords also open and close when you swallow," he explained. "Not only was I unable to make any sound, I also felt I was constantly in danger of drowning in my own saliva. I was assured by the experts that this was permanent. They said, 'It's never coming back. Let it go. Learn to cope.'"

———∞∞∞———

Six months later Jason had learned to cope. He'd learned to communicate with Tausha by whistling his responses to simple questions. He'd undergone another surgery in a long-shot attempt to restore function to his arm. It failed, so he went on enduring electrical sensations "like grabbing hold of a live wire," which are common as nerve endings in paralyzed limbs slowly die away.

He wasn't bitter at the thought that his career, and his passion for performing music, was a thing of the past. That's because he could never quite convince himself it was *true*. "I didn't believe it," he said. "I don't mean to sound arrogant or prideful, but I never really went to that place of massive despair or hopelessness. I remember once trying that on like a coat, and it just didn't fit. I've always felt that things just are the way they are with no one to blame, especially not God. The important question is what are you going to *do* about it?"

—⊗∞⊗—

One morning, sitting in bed before rising for the day, Jason did something about his predicament that surprised even him. Without giving it much thought, he opened his mouth and said, "Hello."

And, just like that, his ability to speak "returned." It wasn't as if he could sing opera that very day, and at first he approached what had happened with "cautious optimism." The sounds he made, crude at first, improved daily with exercise. The truth was undeniable: What medical science told him was gone forever, God gave him back. Within two months he was singing again.

Today he's a professional singer *and* a motivational speaker. He shares this simple message:

"Yes, it was a healing. But it wasn't like a light switch turning on. I know some people are healed instantly like that. I think God did it this way for me—slowly and painstakingly—so I could encourage people to keep believing even if they don't leap up out of a wheelchair or have their cancer disappear overnight. It reinforces the hope that anybody can be well and whole. If God did this for me, then he can do it for you, too. Have faith."

17

FOR THE LOVE OF KRISTIN

Richard and Helen Myers learned that miracles don't have to be "big" to speak volumes about divine grace.

Richard and Helen Myers knew what it was like to have money. Back when Richard had a successful career in the advertising business they never worried about their next paycheck, much less the next meal. Putting food on the table was a matter of a trip to the grocery store and handing over a check. Provision was the predictable product of hard work and responsibility.

That was before a weekend church retreat in the mid-1970s changed everything and put them on a path to learn *God's* idea of provision and the true meaning of "daily bread"—or, rather, the miracle of daily sour cream.

Richard and Helen were raised in Christian homes, but after starting their own family they each desired to go deeper in their faith than ever before. After rededicating their lives to God at the retreat, their spiritual longing turned into a full-fledged calling to full-time ministry. After much prayer, Richard gave up his partnership in a New Jersey agency to join the ministry team of a prominent national evangelist as the organization's business manager. With their young daughter, Kristin, they packed up and headed all the way to Escondido, California.

"It was a big leap for us," he recalled. "But we knew we were right where God wanted us to be."

Well, almost. Not long after their dramatic move, the evangelist decided to scale back the scope of his ministry, eliminating the need for a dedicated manager. Sooner than expected the young couple faced another momentous decision: either return to the relative security of the business world and seek another ministry job in a supporting role, or follow God further into an adventure of surrender and trust—and become evangelists themselves. They quickly recognized there was nothing to decide. God had brought them this far to set the stage for their ministry, and there was no turning back.

But that didn't mean their mailbox instantly filled with offerings and donations. They worked long hours to arrange speaking opportunities and develop new relationships with churches around the country, yet at first their progress was glacial and their situation precarious.

"Finances were extremely tight for us," Richard said. "We had no jobs. Meetings were few and far between. We were in survival mode, totally dependent on God for everything. I mean *everything.*" From the very beginning they made up their minds to trust God alone for provision and never let others know of their specific needs. "That way we'd always know it was *his* doing and not just because we'd asked someone else for help."

For the first time in their married life, Helen had to work extra hard to make their meager groceries stretch far enough for dinner every night. Potatoes—always cheap, nutritious, and filling—became a familiar part of nearly every meal. Not that she and Richard minded much. They would offset culinary monotony with large helpings of gratitude that they had food at all.

But the opinion of six-year-old Kristin was a different matter. Getting her to eat yet another spud almost every night without complaint was a growing challenge. Finally Helen modified a Mary Poppins trick and used a spoonful of sour cream to make the potatoes go down.

One night, with money completely gone and a grocery trip out of the question, she used the last dollop of the blessed topping for Kristin's dinner, scraping the container's bottom to get the last ounce. Without thinking, she tossed it back into the fridge.

The next night she did the same, using a spoon to scoop out every last bit of sour cream onto her daughter's potatoes. She remembers that the top of the container was covered in the yellowed layer that forms when sour cream goes past its prime. Beneath it was just enough fresh cream for the night's meal, and again she mindlessly returned it to the fridge.

By the third night, Helen began to notice the goings-on of something strange. The bottom of the container once again yielded exactly the right amount of sour cream to satisfy Kristin. This time she put it back in the refrigerator on purpose, perplexed by the mealtime mystery.

"It went on like that for three weeks," she said. "We'd have potatoes three or four nights a week, and each time I'd take that sour cream out of the refrigerator there'd be just enough in the bottom for Kristin. I didn't even tell Richard for a while because I didn't have any idea what was going on and was afraid it would dry up."

Eventually she did bring him in on her sour cream secret. Then each night they would both look into the container, still yellow and beyond use around the top, and see exactly what they needed for another meal in the bottom. They recognized the parallel between their encounter and the Old Testament story of the widow's oil jar that never ran dry after Elijah prayed for her provision (see 1 Kings 17).

"That experience touched our hearts deeply," Richard said, "simply because of God's love for a six-year-old. When he cares about a little girl so much that he'd make sure there was enough sour cream for her potatoes, that's a pretty awesome God."

In time a love offering arrived, and Helen went shopping. That night she opened the miraculous container, looked inside, and wasn't a bit surprised to see nothing but a dried and useless crust all the way to the bottom.

"That became the first of many bona fide miracles in our lives and in our ministry," Richard said. "It taught us that miracles aren't always big and flashy. But they always have God's loving fingerprints all over them."

18

"DARLIN'"

*Linda (Dunn) Sasser knows firsthand
that time is no obstacle for God.*

NOVEMBER 17, 2008—ON A RANCH NEAR KERRVILLE, TEXAS

Joe Cantu gave his Caterpillar 262 Skid Steer Loader more throttle as it pushed against an entrenched cedar thicket. Ranchers in the Texas hill country fought constantly to keep their land free of the trees, an exotic species that starved valuable pastureland of water and space. Even above the roar of the big Cat's diesel engine, he heard the snap of branches breaking and roots giving way.

He glanced at his watch. The project was ahead of schedule. A few more minutes and he'd break for lunch.

Then he saw something different on the ground ahead that broke the monotony of prickly pear cactus, dry grass, and cedar. The small area, just a few square yards, had less vegetation and darker soil than the surrounding terrain. Intrigued, he idled the 'dozer and stepped down for a closer look. Something about the scene seemed familiar. He knelt and saw small bits of charred and twisted metal strewn across the dusty surface, none of them larger than a dinner plate. Joe knew instantly what he'd found. He marveled that of all the 'dozer drivers in Texas, *he* was hired to clear this particular patch. How many had been trained by the U.S. Air Force to investigate Vietnam War–era aviation accidents? In fact, while in the Air Force, Joe's job had been to pick up debris from crash sites. Now he knew this bit of discolored earth had a secret to tell: An aircraft had crashed here.

He carefully sifted through the smaller debris and was astonished at the find: the blackened back of a wristwatch and its thin metal face, numbers barely visible; an inch-long segment of the flexible metal wristband; two coins, a nickel and a quarter; and finally, a man's gold wedding ring, tarnished but undamaged.

He brushed off the ring and rubbed the inside of the band. Holding it into the sunlight, Joe read the inscription:

"June 14, 1969." Plus one word: *"Darlin'"*

JUNE 14, 1969—LA MIRADA, CALIFORNIA

Linda Farmer adjusted her veil in the mirror one last time. Her dream was about to come true. In a few minutes she would walk down the aisle of the La Mirada Methodist Church and become Mrs. Larry Dunn. It was a happily-ever-after ending to a storybook romance that began with a young woman's concerned letters to a soldier at war.

"In 1967 I was a student at Cerritos Community College," she recalled. "Just about every day I'd see young men I knew get drafted into the military and leave for Vietnam. When it happened to a close friend, I told him I would be happy to write to anyone who needed letters from home. He was assigned to the 101st Airborne Division, where he met Larry—who just happened to be from my hometown! Over the next year Larry and I wrote many sweet letters back and forth. That's what started our loving relationship."

In Vietnam, Larry served as a door gunner on a Chinook helicopter. He was awarded a Purple Heart when the chopper was shot down over enemy territory during troop redeployment. After his yearlong tour of duty, in September 1968, Larry left the service and returned home. He enrolled at Fullerton Community College to study business. And after a brief person-to-person courtship with his former pen pal, he proposed.

Now he waited for her at the altar in a crisp white jacket and black bow tie. He'd lost none of his upright military posture and demeanor.

Seeing him there, Linda was sure she'd made the right choice—and that she'd spend the rest of her life with him. When the proper moment came, she happily slid a ring onto his finger, one she had secretly inscribed with the pet name she used for him: *"Darlin'."*

December 10, 2008—Kerrville, Texas

Betty Hendricksen went early to her mailbox and found the first installment of her brand-new subscription to the *Hill Country Community Journal,* a recently launched weekly paper devoted to local news in the rugged region west of San Antonio. The story on the front page immediately caught her eye: A local rancher had found a wedding ring in the thirty-six-year-old wreckage of a military helicopter crash. The ring and other artifacts had been turned over to Sheriff Rusty Hierholzer, who, after a little detective work, was convinced it had belonged to Sgt. Bruce Laurence Dunn of Anaheim, California. The article was part of his search for next of kin. "I would like to be able to get the wedding ring back to the family," he'd told the reporter.

"It grabbed my heart!" Betty said. "I'd been researching our family history and had good success tracking down living relatives we didn't even know existed. I went straight to my computer and searched the ancestry.com family trees for the name in the article, and there it was!"

Excited, she sent an email, via an anonymous connection service, to the person who'd posted Larry's name. Then she called Rusty's office to share what she'd found.

MARCH 1, 1972—CORPUS CHRISTI, TEXAS

Larry Dunn was on top of the world, and with good reason. He was close to graduating with an associate's degree in business; he'd been accepted into a training program to become a sheriff's deputy near Los Angeles; and in a few months he would celebrate three years of being married to Linda, the woman whose "letters from home" had stolen his heart all the way over in Vietnam. To top it all off, he was still flying in helicopters—now without getting shot at!

Shortly after marrying Linda, he'd joined an army reserve unit in Van Nuys. The one-weekend-a-month commitment provided a steady income source and kept him in the air a bit longer. When the opportunity arose to return to active duty for a weeklong special assignment to Texas, he jumped at it. The mission: Transport four newly refurbished Huey helicopters from Corpus Christi to Van Nuys. He'd be part of a two-man crew on one aircraft.

"He loved to fly in helicopters," Linda said. "I'm sure he

was there to sign up before the ink was even dry on the request form."

The first leg would take them as far as El Paso, where they planned to spend the night. The preflight inspections had given them no cause for alarm. The aircraft were fueled and cleared for takeoff. After several hours in flight, the monotonous coastal plains below had finally given way to low limestone hills covered in live oak and cedar. Larry was right where he wanted to be.

Then, without warning, the rear rotor on his Huey detached from the tail. The pilot no longer had control, and the helicopter went down in the Texas hills. Loaded with fuel for the long trip, the wreckage immediately burst into flames. All aboard died instantly.

DECEMBER 10, 2008—CHINO HILLS, CALIFORNIA

Melinda's first reaction upon receiving Betty Hendricksen's email was skepticism. She'd seen enough examples of clever online schemes to distrust just about everything. She'd subscribed to the ancestry.com service only a couple of months earlier and wasn't sure what to expect. Still, there was something intriguing about the message:

"Was your Bruce Laurence Dunn killed in a helicopter crash near Kerrville, TX, on 1 March 1972? Our local newspaper has an article today on the front page trying to locate the next of kin, because his wedding ring was found at the crash site. . . . The paper said his wife's name was Linda S. Dunn. The ring has an inscription on it."

"Dunn" certainly had been her stepmother's name before she married Melinda's father, Bob Sasser, thirty-three years before. Melinda was three when they met, and Linda was the only mother she'd ever known. *This is probably some sort of hoax,* she thought. *Wait and see.*

But she didn't have to wait long. Before the day ended, two more emails landed in her inbox, then four more the following day—all from people in Texas who'd seen news coverage of the sheriff's search and wanted to help.

Melinda consulted her brother, Robert, who lived in Florida. After his own initial disbelief, he searched online for the news coverage and found it. Then he called Sheriff Hierholzer to verify the story. It was true! Knowing the news would come as a shock to her mother, Melinda suggested she and Robert contact her together, by conference call.

DECEMBER 12, 2008—PARK CITY, UTAH

Linda was at work at the Christian Center when she got the call. Her heart raced when she realized both her daughter and her son were on the line. What could that mean? *Probably bad news,* she thought. Then Melinda spoke:

"Mom, a rancher in Texas found what they think is Larry's wedding ring. It has an inscription—"

"Darlin'," Linda whispered, unhesitatingly, her heart now in her throat.

In thirty-three years of marriage to Bob Sasser, she had never allowed the pain of her interrupted life with Larry to influence her love for her new family. The story of her previous marriage and how it ended was no secret, but neither was it something she dwelled on. Now, to hear Melinda speak Larry's name aloud after so many years, and to mention a ring she thought was lost forever—it was as if he'd reached out and touched her across time.

"Larry was my first love, and you never forget your first love," she said. "I cried on the phone. I was aware that my children were seeing proof of my love for a man who wasn't their father. But I couldn't help it. I fell apart, out of grief and gratitude. Right away, I knew it was a message from God. It was like he said to me, 'It's okay. Larry's with me.'"

—⁓—

The ring and other items arrived from Texas on December 17, 2008.

"Sheriff Rusty sent the ring with such care," Melinda recalled. "Mom was too nervous to open it, so Dad unwrapped it with great respect and had it all laid out for her when she got home from work. He was there when she needed him the most. For them to go through this together has been very healing for Mom."

Linda wore the ring about a month, and then placed it lovingly in her jewelry box, still overcome with gratitude for the miracle of God's loving grace. In her Christmas letter that year, Melinda told the story to friends and family:

> A devastating time of grief has been turned into a story of hope and faith, 36 years later. If even one of the pieces to this puzzle was not present, it would not be complete: It took the love of marriage vows, a life tragically lost, a beautiful lady keeping her faith through her pain, a rancher's amazing discovery, a sheriff's unfaltering determination, a Texas community willing to get involved, and the love and support of a close family. How would all those pieces fit without God's hand?

Postscript: Around lunchtime on November 17, 2008—just as Joe Cantu had stepped down from the cab of his bulldozer to inspect shiny objects in the dirt—Linda (Dunn) Sasser was traveling thirty thousand feet over his head in a passenger jet. She was on her way home after attending her grandmother's one-hundredth-birthday celebration in Palestine, Texas.

19

AN APPOINTMENT WITH THE GREAT PHYSICIAN

*With her life hanging in the balance, Gracie Rummel
received help from a supernatural source.*

Gracie sprawled on the bench overlooking the community pool. Her brothers Ethan, five, and Nicholas, seven, were having a blast on the water slide, and her mother had tried in vain to coax Gracie onto the steps of the pool. But Gracie just lay on the bench wrapped in her towel. Odd behavior for almost any three-year-old, but very disturbing for this one, a little fish who loved everything about the water.

"How's your breathing, Gracie?" Robin asked.

Gracie had been short of breath lately. Robin, an ER physician, had taken Gracie twice to the hospital to be checked by her colleagues. But Gracie, outgoing and extroverted, had perked up each time she was around the hustle-bustle of the hospital. And each time, the doctors evaluating Gracie had concluded that she appeared perfectly healthy.

But Robin suspected something was wrong. Now, seeing Gracie's poolside lethargy, she was more convinced than ever.

"C'mon, let's head home." She waved the boys out of the water. "Ready, Gracie? Let's go home."

Gracie climbed out of the chair and headed toward the gate. Suddenly she sat down on the cement. "I can't," she said breathlessly. "I'm too tired."

Robin took Gracie back to the ER. This time she was admitted to the pediatric ward. That night, Robin's husband, Tim, stayed home with the boys while she spent the night next to Gracie's hospital bed. The child's heart was racing and she was complaining that her belly hurt. By that point, she hadn't urinated in almost twenty-four hours. She was also gradually becoming less and less responsive.

When the nursing staff hesitated to call Gracie's pediatrician in the middle of the night, Robin called her husband, Tim, also a physician.

"Tim, I think Gracie's dying. You need to get hold of John and get him over here."

Tim reached John Bascom, who was at Gracie's side by six that morning. By then she was being moved to the ICU. She was showing signs of being in shock, but from what? Where was it coming from?

Listening to Gracie's heart, Dr. Bascom heard something amiss. "Before we do a CT scan of her abdomen," he said, "let's get an echocardiogram of her heart."

Robin stood with John as they looked at the scanned images of Gracie's heart. She could see right away that Gracie's heart was barely pumping. "Where's her heart?" Robin said, torn between her roles as mother and doctor. "Nothing's moving."

It turned out Gracie had contracted viral myocarditis, caused by a virus that settles in the muscles of the heart, making it thicken and stiffen until the heart can't pump anymore. Because Gracie's heart wasn't pumping normally, there wasn't enough blood pressure for her other organs to function well. Her stomach didn't digest food normally, which is why her belly hurt and she couldn't eat, and her kidneys weren't getting enough blood pressure to eliminate fluids properly. As a result, fluids her body would normally eliminate built up in her body, leaking into her tissue and skin.

Of children and adults who contract viral myocarditis, a third die, a third need a heart transplant, and a third go on to experience partial to full recovery.

Grasping what Gracie faced, Robin fought back waves of nausea. There was a sense of relief in finally knowing what was wrong, but also a sense of hopelessness in the face of such a devastating a diagnosis.

The next day doctors determined that, with Gracie's body saturated with fluid, they couldn't administer medications through an IV. Instead, they would have to utilize a peripherally inserted central (PIC) line, which led into Gracie's heart cavity in order to drain fluids and administer meds.

Even though Robin had done this procedure countless times on her own patients, she couldn't bear to be in the room. Tim had arrived by then and was there holding Gracie's hand as Robin stepped into the hallway. She was so thankful for his steady, gentle presence, just as she was grateful for such an intelligent doctor who had hurried to Gracie's side and quickly diagnosed the problem. She felt blessed to live in America where her daughter could get good medical care.

But she still felt overwhelmed and grief-stricken, knowing that Gracie was likely to die.

Family and friends began to rally. Tim and Robin's pastor, Matt Heard, from Woodman Valley Chapel in Colorado Springs, came to Gracie's room in ICU, anointed her with oil, and prayed over her. Robin's dad and stepmom arrived from out of town to stay with Ethan and Nicholas while Robin sat with Gracie, and Tim divided his time between home, Gracie, and his medical practice. Robin's sister arrived and simply sat for days with Robin in ICU, a courageous gift since she had recently lost her seventeen-day-old son to a sudden infection.

At the end of that week, Gracie was still alive. Physicians sent her home attached to a monitor, on oxygen, and with sixteen different medications to try to keep her fluids at a level that wouldn't interfere with her digestive tract, her kidneys, and her heart. The doctors were adamant: If Gracie caught so much as a cold, she would die. Colorado was experiencing a horrible influenza epidemic that winter, so it would be a challenge keeping her well. But Robin and Tim were fiercely determined.

When six-year-old Ethan came down with influenza and a temperature of 105, Robin quarantined him to one side of the house and Gracie to the other. For weeks, she donned gown and gloves to attend to her children, so she didn't expose Gracie to Ethan's influenza or get sick herself.

When Ethan recovered, Tim and Robin pulled both boys out of public school so she could homeschool them. To try to save Gracie's life, the family put themselves in quarantine, rarely leaving the house lest anyone bring home a virus or bug that would, literally, be the death of Gracie. Even Dr. Bascom visited Gracie at home rather than have the fragile toddler risk a trip to his office.

The only time Gracie left was when her monitor showed her fluid levels to be so high that her medications wouldn't absorb through her stomach, and she had to go to the hospital to be given meds through her central line.

———

But Gracie didn't respond well. Even in the midst of the most attentive care, she continued to decline, retaining dangerous levels of fluid. Trips to the hospital increased. She barely ate and lost even more weight. If she lay down, fluid would fill her lungs and she would drown, so she slept in a crib next to her parent's bed, propped up on pillows and wearing a monitor that would sound if she slipped into a horizontal position.

One day Robin got a call from Gracie's cardiologist, Dr. Duster, who said, "There's a study at the University of Denver. They're using a beta blocker and having good results with adults with myocarditis. It's helping hearts to develop healthy muscle tissue. They're just now taking a look at the drug's impact on kids. I'd like to enroll Gracie."

Robin and Tim quickly agreed. It was the first bit of good news in three months, ever since that day at the pool when Robin knew without a doubt that something was terribly wrong.

———

Initially Gracie was accepted, and her blood pressure was strong enough to continue. Physicians tried three times, but each time she was dropped from the program. She was, in fact, too sick to participate in a program that might give them a fighting chance to save her life.

Dr. Duster wasn't willing to give up. He went to a pharmacy, instructing the staff to compound a child's dose of the drug specifically for Gracie. She was no longer part of the study, but she continued to take the medication. Still, she continued to go downhill. Nothing seemed to be helping.

One Friday evening Robin was getting ready to leave the cardiologist's office with Gracie when the doctor said gently, "Look, Robin, your whole family has been quarantined and under a lot of stress for months now. The flu season is over, and the risk of Gracie catching something is much lower. Gracie's not improving. But you have today. You can lose this time you have with her by sitting around and worrying, or you can enjoy the time you have. I'm asking you to get Tim and the boys and go out to dinner tonight. Just have a normal family night together."

They were bittersweet words. But that night Tim and Robin piled the boys in the backseat, strapped Gracie in her car seat, and headed to their favorite Mexican restaurant.

Halfway there, Gracie announced, "Mommy, I had a dream last night."

"Really?" Robin said. "What was the dream?"

"I dreamed that my heart broke, and it broke like this—" She made a breaking gesture with her hands.

Tim and Robin both responded, saying what a sad dream that was.

Robin added, "Then what happened?"

"Well, no one could put it back together," she said. "So the angels started crying, 'Waa, waa, waa.'" With balled-up fists, she wrung her hands in front of each eye, to show what the crying angels looked like.

"Was that the end of your dream?" Robin asked.

Gracie perked up and said excitedly, "Oh, no. God came then, and he gave me a new heart. And the angels said, 'Yippee!'"

That night Gracie's monitor went off. She had no blood pressure and her fluid levels had climbed. Drowning in her own fluids, she was admitted to ICU. The next day, after a round of tests, doctors broke the news. "We're not going to get recovery. Gracie's going to need a heart transplant."

Robin and Tim met with specialists at the Children's Hospital in Denver. But there was more bad news. Gracie couldn't be listed for a heart transplant because she was still losing weight. The doctors agreed to see her again in a few weeks in the hope that Tim and Robin could find a way to get her weight to stabilize in that period of time.

After months of watching her daughter hover between life and death, Robin's strength and stamina were stretched to the breaking point. One night she read her Bible, looking for any answers or comfort—any thread of hope. She turned to God in anguished prayer. "I just need to know one way or another what's going to happen to Gracie," she pleaded. "And most of all, I need to know that you are here and that I can trust you with this child."

Tears streaming down her face, she confessed, "I feel that if I leave her for one moment, you'll take her away. I need to know she's safe with you, whether she stays with me or you take her." She finally fell into an exhausted sleep across her Bible.

At 4:00 AM, her cell phone rang. It was a woman friend who said, "Robin, I want you to know that God woke me up and wants you to know he's heard your prayer."

When Robin hung up, she felt amazed—and not nearly as alone as she'd felt just a few hours earlier. God had heard her anguished prayer, confirmed by her friend's out-of-the-blue call.

Around 10:00 that morning, the doorbell rang. Robin opened the door to find a woman from down the street who said, "I wanted you to know that I got two of my girlfriends together and we've been doing energy work around Gracie."

Robin shook her head. "I appreciate your concern for Gracie, I really do, but you know I'm a Christian and I don't feel comfortable with that. I don't feel comfortable with the powers you're calling on."

The woman waved her hand. "Wait. Just hear me out. In the spirit realm, we tried to get near to Gracie, but we couldn't. She was being held in this bright white light, and we couldn't get anywhere near her. My two friends had the same experience. You know I'm not a Christian, but my friends and I talked about it, and the only thing we can conclude is that she's being held in the hands of God."

God was finally getting through to Robin. He hadn't abandoned Gracie. He hadn't abandoned Robin or Tim or the boys. Whatever was going to happen, God would take care of Gracie.

Two nights later, Ethan asked, "Mommy, how do we know Gracie is getting all her medicines?"

"I put a chart on the fridge and check it off," Robin explained.

"How do we know she's getting enough oxygen?"

Robin explained how Gracie's oxygen system worked.

"Mommy, how do we know she's not going to die?"

Robin looked deep into her son's eyes. "Ethan, we don't know. But we know she's not going to die today. And tomorrow, God will give us whatever strength we need."

Robin knew that without God meeting her in a very real way two days earlier, she could never have answered Ethan's question the way she did.

Their very next trip to see the cardiologist up in Denver about Gracie's transplant, the doctor decided Gracie's weight had stabilized. He was willing to put her on the list for a new heart.

Then he took an EKG, and what he saw changed everything. "You know, I'm seeing something here. Her electrical activity is moving in the right direction. It looks like something's happening. I'm going to hold off putting her on the list to see if her heart is going to continue to heal itself."

Over the following months, Robin continued taking Gracie to Denver to see the doctors. Each time they made the trip, Gracie would ask, "Why are we going there?"

"To talk to the doctors about getting you a new heart," she would answer.

Every time, Gracie responded, "You can talk to the doctors, Mommy, but I told you, God already gave me a new heart."

—⚬⚬⚬—

Gracie's heart continued to get stronger. Eight months later, she was weaned off all medications. That September, she started preschool.

When she was six, her cardiologist lifted all physical restrictions. That meant Gracie's echocardiogram confirmed she was strong enough to do anything she wanted. He told Robin, "Swimming is the last activity I add for a kid who's had heart trouble. But Gracie's heart is strong enough to handle it." A few weeks later, Gracie went swimming for the first time in three years.

In three more years, when she was nine, Gracie was given a clean bill of health. They were in Dr. Duster's office when he said, "She's completely normal. All residual thickening of the wall of her heart is completely gone. There's absolutely no sign of anything irregular with her heart chambers at all. You know," he added, "this just doesn't happen. Not in cases as serious as Gracie's. This is a miracle."

Robin says that there wasn't a miraculous *moment* in which Gracie was healed. She says, instead, that it was a miraculous *journey*.

Today, Gracie is twelve. She plays competitive soccer. Her parents remind her often, "You know, Gracie, you never questioned that God had given you a new heart. And he had. It just took some time for us to see it."

20

"You Will Not Die"

It took around seventeen months for Willie Beeson to lose everything. It took a few moments in heaven to get it all back.

In March 2005, on Palm Sunday in Southern California, Willie Beeson grimaced in pain as he transferred from car to wheelchair in the Diamond Bar Community Center parking lot. He'd come at his brother's invitation for prayer from the pastors of Father's House Church, a brand-new congregation.

For over a year his family had watched Willie descend from the prime of his life—active, healthy, successful as a heating and air-conditioning contractor—into a ghost of his former self. If Job's story were written as a contemporary account of hardship, pain, and loss, it might tell Willie's tale.

Inexplicably, five back surgeries since December 2003 *each* had left him worse off than before. He languished in a dense fog of hopeless despair.

His first reaction to his brother's invitation had been anger. "I was very frustrated with Harry and told him I wouldn't go," he recalled. "Why did he think this praying and laying-hands-on stuff worked? I'd heard of many people getting their hopes up only to still be in pain or dead after the excitement wore off."

Besides, Willie had already decided to die. What was the point of prayer?

Then, however, he reconsidered. He reasoned that it might provide some comfort and closure to his family to gather and pray for him. His wife, Darla, and their three children had suffered all these months, too. She deserved a "real" husband, not a "lump of meat." His kids deserved a dad who could care for them suitably. Suddenly a prayer service seemed appropriate—it could serve as a sort of emotional dress rehearsal for his long-overdue funeral.

———

Pastors laid hands on Willie and asked God to heal him of his injuries, to restore him to health, and to give back all he had lost. Everyone in the room prayed along in agreement—everyone except Willie, whose own prayer remained unchanged: *"Please, let me die."*

Instantly a bright light filled the room, and he heard a voice say, "You will not die." Then the light faded and was gone. It was obvious nobody else had seen or heard anything. Now he felt *angry*. Like Job, he wondered why he'd ever been born.

———

On Father's Day 2002, Willie injured his back in a four-wheeler accident in the California desert. The damage was serious but didn't require surgery, just plenty of rest. Progress was slow and frustrating, yet in February 2003, he started the right regimen of physical therapy and worked with a personal trainer. By the end of the year, he'd completed a series of treatments with a specialized chiropractic machine designed to strengthen his injured lower back region. He'd lost fifty pounds and regained much of his strength and flexibility.

Then, as one doctor would put it, Willie "stepped out of a disaster into a catastrophe." On the last day of treatment with the machine, during one final exercise, the spinal disc between the L4 and L5 vertebrae ruptured.

In a flash his reality rapidly spiraled into escalating and blinding pain.

Here's a compressed timeline of what happened next. . . .

———∞∞∞———

December 23, 2003. After surgery to repair the rupture, his doctor calls it "the biggest I've ever seen." The surgeon says they must wait at least three weeks for another MRI to allow swelling to subside. But Willie's pain level is so great he changes his mind, ordering the scan on December 30. Shocked to discover that another rupture has occurred, he schedules another surgery.

January 2, 2004. After the four-hour second procedure, his left leg is numb; he describes his pain level as 9+ out of 10. *Morphine* has little effect.

January 5, 2004. A new MRI reveals that formation of a hematoma—a large "blood balloon"—in the spinal canal is causing the severe pain, pressing on the L4 nerve root. The doctor, visibly worried, schedules emergency surgery for the following day and advises Willie and Darla there's a good chance the procedure will leave his leg paralyzed.

January 6, 2004. The surgery is a "success," but after three operations in two weeks, Willie's pain is so severe he has trouble breathing. Maximum medication levels provide little relief. His leg is still numb.

January 9, 2004. Willie is released from the hospital. Severe pain has subsided somewhat but massive med doses continue. The doctor is hopeful that the worst is over.

Throughout January and February, though, his pain level continues to worsen. He's become completely addicted to morphine and other drugs. In his journal he writes, "I am a tough guy, but with my stamina low and my nerves shot, the pain just hits with such intensity. If it weren't for the pain med, I would be thinking suicide, I'm sure."

August 3, 2004. Willie and Darla travel to Germany for an "artificial disc replacement," a procedure not yet approved in the United States. After much research, Willie is certain this will bring relief at last.

August 7, 2004. The surgery *is* successful. For the first time in months, he can walk easily. What's more, he's virtually pain-free. In post-op he progresses quickly and is released to go home, two days ahead of schedule.

One evening, in the hotel restaurant, he bends over and is struck by pain. It passes; doctors conclude the replacement disc is undergoing "subsidence," a common occurrence and no cause for alarm. Willie and Darla head home.

When they land in LA, Willie goes straight to the hospital. His abdomen is severely bloated due to a surgery-related condition called seroma—dangerous fluid leakage putting pressure on his organs. Upon examination, domestic doctors decide that the artificial disc is too small for him and the "subsidence" is unlikely to improve. By late September, still waiting for FDA approval to remove the disc, doctors declare it's too late to do so safely.

October 23, 2004. Willie returns to Germany for "two weeks of hell." The bottom line: During disc replacement surgery, Willie suffers a collapsed femoral artery in his left leg. The pain is beyond anything he's experienced so far.

November 5, 2004. Within hours of arriving back in California, pain is so severe that his blood pressure rockets to 225/100. After five surgeries and two trips to Germany, Willie is readmitted with no remaining viable options and a most uncertain future. On top of all else, he has developed gallstones and is scheduled for yet another operation to remove them.

March 2005. Willie's business partners invoke an obscure clause in the corporate agreement, declare him "incapacitated," and seize his shares in the company. The move also puts his health insurance in jeopardy.

"The last thing I had left was ownership in that business," he said. "I was now stripped as naked as the day I was born, no use to anyone. I truly was an emotionally, mentally, physically, and spiritually broken man."

The night of the prayer service just a few days earlier, when Willie heard a voice declaring that he would not die, he'd picked up Darla's Bible off the bed to move it out of the way. As he tossed it aside, the pages flipped open to Psalm 143. His eyes were drawn to verse 8: "Let the morning bring me word of your unfailing love, for I have put my trust in you." He read on for a few more lines, still angry and confused. He set the book down.

Later he picked it up again. Again it opened to that page. In the following days he read the same psalm over and over.

But he saw no reason to change what he'd prayed while others asked for healing. *"Please, let me die."*

———⊗⊗⊗———

April 26, 2005, 3:00 AM. Willie heads to bed after several hours of writing in his journal and reading in another room, giving Darla a chance to sleep. As he sits on the edge of the bed, he feels a "pressure" in his consciousness, "like wind blowing." Suddenly he's no longer in his room. Surrounded by darkness, he sees a radiant golden gate in the distance and is being drawn rapidly toward it. Two pillars like giant elephant tusks rise high in the air, arching toward each other in the center but without touching. Two glimmering gates hang beneath them without any visible support. The gates are open.

He observes that he's been "traveling" on a road leading up to the gates and beyond. It's at least a quarter mile wide and made of "liquid, translucent gold," the purest, most beautiful thing he's ever seen. The road is strewn with precious jewels in every imaginable color: rubies, sapphires, emeralds, diamonds.

He becomes aware of music. Many voices sing a melody that fills him with an "unbelievable sense of peace and serenity." Then he sees that the road is lined on each side by thousands upon thousands of people: a diverse crowd of men, women, and children dressed in brilliant garments made of light. Some play long golden trumpets and other instruments. The rest sing.

"It's like the music was coming through me," he recalled. "I was hearing it, but telepathically, through every fiber of my being. Nothing on earth compares to the perfection of that sound."

Beyond the gates he sees a dazzling white city, filled with radiant buildings and bustling people and other creatures.

He can't look directly at it; the light is too bright and over-powering. But he senses a force flowing from the center of the city, the source of everything he sees. It is the most powerful *love* conceivable.

"In this life, we can never quite put our finger on who we are and where we're supposed to be," he said. "Seeing the city and feeling the infinite power of that love, I knew: *This is where we're supposed to be*. It literally felt like the final puzzle piece was inserted into my mind, like everything lacking was downloaded all at once."

Then he asks himself: *Is this heaven? Am I dead?* He experiences a sudden, rushing replay of his entire life and a preview of things yet to come.

"No, you are not dead," says a voice beside him. "Your destiny is beginning now. Satan's work is done."

Willie turns and sees a "beautiful, radiant man" standing beside him. Pure, powerful love emanates from him, "like he has been my very, very best friend for my whole life."

"Willie Beeson," the being says, "God is blessing you. You will be completely healed, strong, vigorous, and young."

Then Willie is back in his bedroom. He wakes Darla to tell her what he's just experienced. She thinks it's another morphine-induced hallucination and goes back to sleep.

Willie himself is bewildered and confused. The vision seemed so *real*. He records the details in his journal and lies down to sleep.

———

Willie wakes after Darla has left for work. He stands. Immediately he knows that something is different.

First, he has no pain. Second, his left leg is no longer numb. He touches the skin that long has been cold and lifeless. It's warm. He feels blood flowing again. The muscles are firm and healthy. He straightens his back and stands fully erect for the first time in seventeen months.

Excitement and wonder are building as he walks downstairs and out the front door without cane or wheelchair.

"Then I started screaming at the top of my lungs. I took off and ran, jumping and shouting and praising God. I ran for at least a mile through the neighborhood in my pajamas. I'd never felt anything like this. It was way beyond ecstasy."

—— ⊱⊰ ——

One could say Willie hasn't stopped running since. God kept his promise and healed Willie *completely*:

- His back is fully restored. His vertebrae spontaneously fused around the implant, giving him, in the words of one doctor, "a stronger spine than anything medical science could have done."
- His muscle tone throughout his entire body was instantly restored.
- His femoral artery is still "collapsed," according to medical imagery, but the flow of blood in his leg is close to full capacity.
- His gallstones vanished.
- His addiction to maximum doses of pain medication vanished without symptoms of withdrawal.
- His medical bills were paid to the penny by a settlement with the practice where the disc injury occurred.
- He has returned to work in a new business of his own.

"To this day I wonder, *Why me?* I'm not a pastor, not a theologian, just a common person with an uncommon journey," said Willie, whose book, *The Impossible Miracle*, fully details his experience. "I only know that today I'm a different person with a perspective that few achieve in this life. I give thanks to God for his being an unfailing source of freedom from worry and fear of the things of this world. If God could do this for me, he can do it for anyone."

21

A VOICE IN THE WILDERNESS

*Caught in a Colorado blizzard, Marco and
Freddie Alvarez found out just what it means that
God is "an ever-present help in trouble."*

Marco Alvarez had never seen snow like this. The storm descended like a swarm of livid bees, whipped into a frenzy by cold, bitter wind. In a matter of minutes visibility dropped to zero.

Marco, together with his fourteen-year-old son, Freddie—on a long-awaited Colorado hunting trip—had welcomed the first lazy flakes that morning on the mountain ridge near timberline. They'd decided the previous day after scouting the terrain that here the elk were most likely to pass.

The snow was a fitting addition to the father-son adventure they had been planning for months. They hiked to their hiding place in the pale early light, catching flakes on their tongues and enjoying the soft quiet that accompanies a gentle snowfall, a rare treat for the visitors from Phoenix.

They settled in behind a fallen tree trunk to wait. They checked their rifles and listened intently for sounds of an encroaching herd. Nothing. Their breath made clouds of fog in the air. The feeble November sun rose in the sky, but the gloom in the forest only grew darker as time went by. And the snowfall steadily intensified, collecting on their coats and hats.

"We joked about how funny it would be to show up back home looking like two giant snowmen," Marco said. "I'd read all the info I could find about hunting safety beforehand, but nothing prepared me for how fast things can go from postcard perfect to full-blown disaster up in the mountains."

They heard the wind approaching long before they felt it or saw it thrash through the trees. From a distance it sounded like a torrent of rushing water. When it arrived, the air filled instantly with a swirling, biting maelstrom of snow. It stung their eyes and lashed at their exposed faces. The wind chill swiftly caused the apparent temperature to drop more than twenty degrees.

"I signaled Freddie to follow me and headed for the deer trail we'd walked to get there," Marco recalled. "It didn't take long to realize that while we'd been enjoying the winter scenery, the snow had covered the trail completely. We were at least two miles from our campsite, and like Hansel and Gretel, it seemed as though the birds had eaten our bread crumbs."

Marco knew they needed to get away from the treeless slopes just above them and into the forest's relative protection. He also felt confident that with a little luck they would recognize the way they'd come and find their camper trailer.

That confidence didn't last long. Marco couldn't see more than a few feet in any direction, so the landmarks he might have used to navigate were invisible. Snow was piling up at an alarming rate. Progress was slow and halting as they searched for firm footing on the steep, rocky, log-strewn mountainside.

"I hate to say it, Freddie," he said after they'd walked half an hour. "But I think we're lost."

"Let's ask God to help us," Freddie said, after pausing to let his father's assessment sink in.

———∞∞∞———

The storm seemed to grow worse by the minute. The temperature kept falling. They could afford to waste no time. Marco considered his son's suggestion with a bit of skepticism but realized he didn't have a better idea.

He thought of himself as a Christian, mostly in the same way he thought of himself as a Republican or a member of the bowling league. He hadn't grown up in a Christian home himself, but for his wife's sake he made sure his family attended church and that his kids went to Sunday school. He regularly volunteered at church, giving generously of his time and money.

However, the idea that God was present and available in everyday life, to the point of offering real help in times of trouble, was one he'd never quite come to trust. He'd seen—and endured—too much suffering to overcome the notion that God's interest in human life was mostly theological and academic.

Fortunately, Freddie had a different perspective on faith. The previous year the young man had attended a summer church camp in Lake Arrowhead, California, and come back changed. He was less selfish now, less obsessed with video games and TV. He was noticeably more tolerant of his siblings. When it was Freddie's turn to pray at family mealtimes, Marco had the feeling his son was speaking to someone real, not just reciting obligatory words.

Stranded in a blizzard in the unfamiliar Rockies, Freddie said, "Let's ask God for help" as if he planned to use a cell phone and call him up.

So they prayed.

"Dear God," Marco began, trying to sound convincing. "Looks like we're in some trouble and could use your help. Please show us which way to go to find our trailer."

"Lord," Freddie added in an earnest voice. "You know where we are and where we need to get to, but we sure don't. This is scary, and we're trusting you to help us. Amen."

Marco well knew they were surrounded by thousands of square miles of forest. Even in perfect weather, a lost person could search for weeks and not find a tiny campsite tucked into a nondescript valley. But he kept his fears to himself and looked around, shielding his eyes from the stinging snow.

Now would be a good time for you to speak up, God, he thought.

Hearing nothing but howling wind, he chose the most promising course through an opening in the trees and headed toward it.

Just then a strange noise came from his right. He looked and saw a large black raven clinging to the snowy bough of a nearby blue spruce. It cocked its head to one side and looked at them for a long moment. It called again in its mumbling, gravelly voice and flew, low to the ground, away from the direction Marco had chosen. They watched it go, and then, from a distance, the bird called again, barely audible above the driving wind.

"We should go that way," Freddie said matter-of-factly, pointing after it.

Marco started to argue that following birds through the forest was the least likely way to safety. *That's like trying to find your way back to port by following a fish in the ocean,* he told himself. But the look on Freddie's face stopped him short. He motioned for Freddie to lead.

Together they trudged through snow that was nearly a foot high, deeper where the wind pushed it into drifts. The forest had become featureless, a blanket of white snow. Every direction began to look the same, with no clear reason to go one way and not another. Still his son pressed on.

—————— ✖✖✖ ——————

After they had walked an hour or more, Marco was beginning to fear the worst. Suddenly Freddie grabbed his arm and pointed excitedly forward.

In the trees ahead sat the raven, observing them like an ancient mystic. Then Marco looked past the bird, down the hillside through the blowing snow. He laughed aloud when he saw what Freddie must have seen—their trailer just ahead in a familiar clearing. The two whooped and hugged, filled with relief.

As if on cue the raven raised its wings and gave three loud, deep-throated calls. Then it flapped away, over their heads, back the way they had come.

"I knew right then that God had answered our prayer, just like Freddie believed he would," Marco said. "The fact that he used the voice of a raven to do it made it all the more miraculous to me. Now it's easier for me to believe that he is always with us, ready to help, no matter what."

The storm began to abate soon after they were safely inside. By nightfall the sky was clear and calm. The next morning they watched, amazed, as the elk herd passed by silently in glistening snow, a few feet from their window.

"Thank you!" was all either of them could say.

22

LIVE BY THE SWORD

*A life-threatening tumor pushed Greg Kirk to the brink
of death. Divine intervention pulled him back.*

For most of his life, Greg Kirk had handled pain the way
most men do: Ignore it and hope it goes away.

In the spring of 1999, he happened to notice a nagging, persistent pressure in his back. An avid outdoorsman, he
initially assumed he'd pulled a muscle and strained cartilage.
Busy with many responsibilities and wary of doctors anyway,
he believed the discomfort would disappear eventually.

It didn't. And as his back pain worsened, he encountered
other problems, like nasty colds that would come and go almost weekly. Still, he chalked them up to the damp Northern
California storms that would blow inland.

As assistant director of the Union Gospel Rescue Mission
of Sacramento and pastor of Natomas Baptist Church, Greg
put in long hours at the homeless shelter, at the church, and

with his three teenagers. He didn't have time for doctor visits or colds or any such nonsense. Until he got a wake-up call.

—⚬⚬⚬—

Greg and his wife, Pam, rode bikes around the neighborhood every night after dinner as their schedules allowed. And each night Greg, a competitive type, would make sure he got to the garage door first even if by a single knob of his mountain-bike tire. But one particular night as they pedaled toward home, he slowed and then stopped completely. He dismounted and plopped down on the ground, looking as if he were finishing a triathlon instead of a leisurely ride.

Suddenly realizing she was ahead in the contest, Pam turned and called, "Hey, what's going on? It's not like you to give up."

"I don't know," Greg said. "I'm winded—and exhausted. I can hardly breathe. Not sure I can make it." He ended up walking his bike the half mile to home.

Later, he reluctantly described what had happened, along with the back and chest pain he'd been enduring, to his mother-in-law, Patricia. She said, "Son, you need to see a doctor." When his mother-in-law spoke, Greg listened and obeyed.

—⚬⚬⚬—

So it came to be that on April 23, 1999, Greg sat shirtless on an exam table. A physician was running tests, checking his heart with a stethoscope, scribbling notes on a clipboard. As part of a large HMO, Greg had received the runaround until he'd finally landed in an unfamiliar urgent-care center with an unfamiliar doctor who treated him like the next item on the assembly line.

She spent fifteen minutes examining, only occasionally uttering an inscrutable "Hmm." Surely it was nothing serious.

At age thirty-nine, Greg had never faced any significant health crises.

Finally she said, "Well, Mr. Kirk, you have pneumonia." She also noted in passing that one test had shown a blood-gas level of 98 percent, which meant nothing to him at the time. She wrote a prescription for amoxicillin and sent him on his way.

No sweat, he thought. *I'll take it easy for a few weeks and be as good as new.*

The next Monday morning, Greg's workday was interrupted by a call from a doctor he'd never heard of. "I need to see you right away," he said.

Thinking it strange that a physician would phone him directly, Greg promised to make a follow-up appointment.

"I need to see you right away," Dr. Cashman said tersely. "Right *now.*"

Canceling his appointments, Greg hurried to the hospital. Driving over, he thought, *This is a bunch of bunk. These huge HMOs can't keep anything straight. It's probably a big mix-up.*

Sitting in Dr. Cashman's office, Greg heard the man he'd just met say, "You are a very lucky man. The physician on call reviewed your test results from the other night. She's a pulmonary specialist. Twenty other physicians would not have detected the extreme problem you are facing."

Extreme problem? I wouldn't call pneumonia an extreme problem.

The physician continued. "With a blood-gas level of 98 percent, there is no way you have pneumonia. I'm sorry to say you have something much more serious."

"What does 'more serious' mean?"

"We found a nodule on your lung. We need to get you in for tests as soon as possible—X-rays, an MRI, and others."

That day and in the week ahead, Greg followed orders and underwent a series of tests. Unfortunately no one told him the results, *or* anything else. He knew nothing more of his condition than when he initially saw Dr. Cashman.

One thing he knew for sure: His pain was getting worse. Almost daily he felt as if he were having a heart attack: severe pain in his chest, shooting pain down his arm, shortness of breath. Nothing helped but the prescribed Vicodin.

Weeks later, as he tried to refill his prescription at the patient services office, the clerk refused because it was classified as a controlled substance.

"I'm in severe pain," he protested. "I can hardly function without this medication."

She pulled up his file and said, "Sir, have you consulted your surgeon?"

Perplexed, Greg said he didn't know anything about a surgeon.

"It's right here," she informed him. "You're scheduled for surgery."

"Surgery?" He shook his head. "I haven't heard one thing about this."

———— ∞∞∞ ————

He knew it must be urgent the next day when his surgeon walked into the consultation room holding a jumbo-sized container of Vicodin and said, "Here you go, Mr. Kirk. With what you have, I'm not concerned about your abusing prescription drugs. If you get addicted, we can deal with that later."

Growing more alarmed by the second, Greg asked what, in fact, he had.

"Has no one talked to you?" The surgeon paused. "Mr. Kirk, you are facing a thoracotomy. That is the removal of part or all of a lung. Basically we cut you in half and take a tumor out of you."

Suddenly feeling light-headed, Greg tried to listen as the doctor explained.

"You have a large tumor growing inside you. In ten weeks it's grown from a small nodule to ten centimeters—the size of a softball. It's a very aggressive form of cancer. Furthermore, this tumor is lodged between your lung and your heart. One of two things will happen: I'm going to do this surgery, removing a rib and then the tumor and you're going to be fine. Or I'm going to open you up, close you back up, and tell you you've got a year to live."

To top off this devastating news, the surgeon went on. "I've been a vascular surgeon for forty-seven years. I drink, smoke, gamble, run around with women—and I'm healthy as a horse. I look at a person like you who's dedicated his life to helping others, pastoring a church, working with the homeless, and here you have a terrible form of cancer. Tell me, what kind of God does that?"

Stunned by the doctor's audacity, Greg answered, "Listen, sir, I don't know you, and you don't know me. But I can tell you this: God has a reason for everything he does. His will shall be done, no matter what."

He believed every word he'd said. But he couldn't deny his bewildering sense of grief. His ministry, his marriage, his family—it could all be gone. He prayed, *I accept your will, God . . . but I'd sure like to keep on living!*

———❧———

Two weeks later, Greg attended the conference of the Association of Gospel Rescue Missions in Spokane, Washington.

At this annual gathering of more than a thousand global workers, he always drew encouragement from the workshops, the speakers, and his colleagues. Still, he decided not to share the news of his diagnosis. Feeling awkward about how he would tell people and about the fuss they might make, he resolved to quietly express his gratitude to those who had meant so much to him.

One morning, his good friend Jeff Gilman, director of Redwood Gospel Mission in Santa Rosa, California, asked him to walk along the Spokane River. Strolling on the river walk, Jeff stopped abruptly and said, "You're sick, aren't you, Greg."

Dumbfounded, Greg asked how he knew.

"The Lord told me. You haven't shared this with anyone here, but I'm going to pray for your healing."

Greg expressed his appreciation and asked that Jeff keep the news quiet, since he was struggling to process it all himself.

Featured on the conference's third night was Frank Peretti, best-known for his spiritual-warfare-themed novels and also as an accomplished banjo player. He delivered a short talk on God's unconditional love and then gave a concert with his bluegrass band, Northern Cross.

Afterward, Greg decided to say thanks for the message and music. When he mentioned that he too played the banjo, Frank invited him to hang around and jam with the band. He hurried to his room for his instrument and returned a few minutes later to find the band members and other folks casually sitting by the stage, listening to the music or chatting.

Fifteen minutes into their impromptu jam session, Frank suddenly stopped. He closed his eyes and stroked his gray-flecked beard. Then he leaned close to Greg and whispered,

"So how come you're not telling anybody you're sick? The Lord told me you're very sick. We're going to pray for you right now."

The band members gathered around and prayed for Greg. Without another word, Frank took up his banjo again and they resumed their playing.

Again Greg sat dumbfounded. *This is the strangest thing that's ever happened to me,* he thought. *It's mysterious and maybe even miraculous.*

Back at home, Greg felt his spiritual and emotional high receding as he faced tough days ahead. He had more appointments, stacks of hospital and insurance forms to fill out, and a prep workup for the forthcoming operation.

In a pre-op consultation, the surgeon explained: He would attempt to remove the tumor but would take out a rib to access it. If organ damage was a risk, a biopsy would be taken for further tests—with the tumor left in place. In either case, Greg could expect extended rounds of chemotherapy and radiation.

He underwent surgery on June 20 of that year and spent four nights in the hospital, the first two in ICU with breathing tubes. In the middle of his first night there, he woke with a start. Someone was in his room. A brightly illuminated figure stood at the foot of his bed—a towering figure in a robe. Greg couldn't see distinctly enough to determine a gender, and that didn't seem to matter.

The visitor lingered a long while, touching Greg's shoulder and wiping his brow. An overwhelming sense of peace swept over Greg. Though groggy, he knew this was more than a dream.

The next morning, he asked the nurse if someone had come in during the night.

"No one," she replied.

When he insisted *someone* was there, the nurse insisted right back—*no one* came or went after visiting hours.

Then the same thing happened again. The illuminated being brought comfort through the following night. And the next night. When the nurse assured him repeatedly that no one had visited, Greg knew an angel had been sent to him.

On the fourth night, he slept soundly until he woke again to see the figure shining brightly. He watched wide-eyed and awestruck as the angel unsheathed a gleaming sword and plunged it into his side. Instead of pain, astoundingly, Greg felt a soothing sensation.

The angel said, "You have more to do for the Master." The words weren't so much said as they were *conveyed*. Greg received them without hearing them spoken. With that, the angel vanished.

Upon his release, Greg was told that a rib had not been removed. Deeply confused and concerned, he remembered the surgeon saying that leaving the ribs intact meant the tumor couldn't be cut out. In that case, he'd face a grim prognosis. But he clearly recalled the angel's reassuring words and soothing sword.

Finally the surgeon called Greg at home. "I've got great news for you, Mr. Kirk. When I opened you up, I touched your rib. It was as if it was made of rubber. Your ribs just opened up, like another hand went in there making room for the tumor to be removed. I excised it as fast as I've ever done."

And he had more good news: "I can't explain it, but the tumor was benign. I *know* it was malignant before the surgery. You won't need chemo or radiation." The same man who had mocked God for allowing Greg's illness now concluded by saying, "You have an absolutely wonderful God. I have never seen a miracle before in my life, but I've seen one now."

———❧———

All these years later, Greg has had no more health problems. Since 2006 he has served as director of United Gospel Rescue Mission in Poplar Bluff, Missouri. His ministry to the homeless has flourished, as has his marriage and relationship with his now-grown children. He is motivated by the angel's words—"You have more to do for the Master"—as he tries to make the most of the time he's been given.

Reflecting on his experiences, he said, "I was raised a Baptist, with a fairly conservative theological perspective. I'd heard plenty of sermons about angels and even delivered a couple myself. It was pretty theoretical. Frankly, I was skeptical about angels having direct, visible contact with people—until it happened to me. For whatever reason, God chose to perform a miracle in my life. Now I know that every day is a gift, to be used for him."

23

HIS HEART STOPPED ON VALENTINE'S DAY

After Jeff Buchanan suffered a massive coronary, the restoration God granted was surprising and far-reaching.

Monday is pizza night around the Buchanan house, and February 14, 2011, was no exception. But on this day, before the family of five dug into the goods from Little Caesar's, Jeff called his wife, Erica, and their three daughters—Aubrey, fourteen, Emily, ten, and Haley, six—into the kitchen of their Oklahoma City home. He handed each a small bouquet of roses and a box of chocolates decorated with a handwritten note and a paper heart cutout.

After dinner, Erica, retreating to the home office to handle a few things, had to smile at the laughter coming from the other room, where the kids had engaged Jeff in a tickling match. At one point Haley, happy and breathless, ran in and grabbed her mother's phone. "I want to take a picture!" she announced, and Erica barely had time to nod permission before the girl disappeared.

The couple had met nine years earlier when they each returned to college as adults. Erica knew immediately there was something genuine about this kind and charming big bear of a man, and her two daughters—then one and five—seemed to feel the same way. Jeff and Erica married and, two years later, welcomed Haley.

Now this wife and mother couldn't think of a lovelier way to spend Valentine's Day than sharing pizza with her boisterous, happy family.

Twenty minutes after seeing the girls to bed, Erica was wrapping up in the office and getting ready to join her husband when she heard him call from the bedroom. He said one word, "Babe," and she knew something was wrong.

Running in she saw Jeff lying sideways across the bed, gasping for air and speechless. She called 9-1-1, then looked up and saw Aubrey and Emily, wide-eyed and scared, in the doorway. "Go get the neighbors!" she instructed.

Casey and Amber, friends next door, arrived the same time as the EMTs. A paramedic told Amber to keep Erica and the girls in the kitchen while they wheeled Jeff on a stretcher through the living room.

Tears streaming down her face, Erica begged, "What's going on? Why can't I see him?"

Amber said gently, "Erica, he's not breathing. They can't find a pulse. They don't want you or the girls to see him this way."

Don Payne, a nurse, showed up as usual around 6:30 AM Tuesday at Oklahoma Heart Hospital. As he rounded the corner into the CCU and glanced into Room 220, he could tell by the machines and family members' demeanor that the guy was in bad shape. But he was used to that—this was the critical care unit, after all—so it wasn't a shocker until the night nurse handed over his shift report. Regarding this patient he said, "Post-cardiac arrest. Big chill. He's probably not going to make it, and he's thirty-nine."

Then it hit him like a punch in the gut: Don had turned thirty-eight last October, his best friend had died of a heart attack at thirty-seven, and his father had died of cancer at forty-one. Sometimes he felt he was approaching the age when he was living on borrowed time, and here he was, facing a patient his age who was teetering between life and death.

He reviewed his patient's history.

Jeff Buchanan had been admitted after going into sudden cardiac arrest. For an hour and a half he didn't respond to medicine or CPR. He received electrical shocks to his heart twenty times to no avail. Doctors told his family it didn't look good, but that because he was so young they were going to try everything—CPR, meds, shock paddles—once more before calling it quits.

This time the guy's heart started. It wasn't stable, it wasn't pretty, but it was enough to move him into CCU.

At that point he'd gone an estimated fifteen minutes without any blood or oxygen to the brain and ninety minutes without a natural heartbeat. It was expected that he would be a vegetable for the rest of his life. Doctors told the man's sobbing wife and family they wanted to take him into what they called "The Big Chill," bringing his body temp to 91 degrees—into a hypothermic state—to minimize brain damage.

In this fairly new approach, the patient would be sedated so as not to wake during the three-day process, wherein he would remain in a coma and paralyzed so his body could rest and focus on stabilizing his heart and brain. Until the doctors warmed him back up, his family would not be allowed to talk to him or touch him. You didn't want to do anything to stimulate a patient in a big chill. You didn't want him to wake up. Not yet.

—⁂—

By 6:00 AM Tuesday Erica was spent. All night long, doctors and nurses had expected that any moment would be Jeff's last. He was on eighteen drip medications and swimming in a sea of tubes and machines. His liver and his kidneys had stopped working. Just when she thought she'd cried every last tear, she picked up her phone and opened her photo gallery. There was one of Jeff tickling Emily, taken less than an hour before he'd cried out for help. It was the picture Haley had snapped when she'd borrowed the phone. Had they really been so blissfully happy just a few short hours ago? Staring at the snapshot, Erica dissolved into yet another rising tide of tears.

Soon the waiting room was filled with praying friends and family. The hallways were packed. There was even a group of committed friends praying on the sidewalk several floors beneath Jeff's window.

Erica's best friend, Allyson, rarely left her side. Allyson knew she'd never seen anyone so scared, so shaken, or so desperate. The women prayed together throughout the early morning hours.

The doctors told Erica they didn't think Jeff would recover and that if he did he'd have no brain function. Each time they brought bad news, she would say, "Okay, what are the top three things we need to be praying for right now?" Then she'd use Facebook and Twitter to broadcast the requests.

171

Throughout Wednesday, Don monitored Jeff's blood pressure, blood glucose, potassium, and heart rhythm. All levels were either dangerously high or dangerously low, and it was a balancing act between life and death trying to get everything shifted to within a safe range.

Jeff had been in hypothermia twenty-four hours; it was time, over the next twelve, to warm him back up. Once his temperature was normal, they would try to wake him. That's when they would know the extent of his brain damage.

Don had expected that friends and family would arrive to show their support or pray. But he was surprised by the number of people who came and how boldly they asked God to heal Jeff. They seemed to *expect* it to happen.

This was a bittersweet reminder of what Don once had in his own life. Not that long ago he'd been involved in a loving church family and had enjoyed such deeply committed relationships. But as he'd often said, he had placed too much faith in people and not enough in God. Disappointed by certain circumstances within the church, he had slipped away.

Now seeing the love and support poured out on the Buchanans, he felt a stirring in his heart. He missed this love, this kinship. This dependence on God. This vital, active, *living* faith.

He asked Erica where they attended. When she said, "Life Church, in Edmond," he was surprised. It was a big church. How had they developed such intimate friendships in a congregation of that size?

As he pondered, in his spirit he felt a whispered answer, loving but full of truth: "Don, stop underestimating me. Haven't you learned yet that your preconceived ideas about how I work aren't always true?"

He headed home after his shift. He'd settled into his recliner when he got a text: "Just coded 220."

Jeff's heart had stopped.

———∞∞∞———

Erica had been in the waiting room with others when she heard through hallway speakers a code blue call for 220. Immediately she and other family members started running toward Jeff's room. There they could see doctors and nurses working fast and efficiently to try to restart his heart. Erica collapsed.

Within several minutes the medical team had his heart started and stabilized. Attention turned to Erica. Allyson and a nurse got her into a chair, and Allyson urged, "Stay strong. Jeff needs you." Then she ran to tell everyone Jeff was stable but to keep praying.

Around midnight his temp was normal. It was time to try waking him up.

Now something suddenly snapped for Erica. Before, she'd been fighting for her husband, yet she'd also been sorrowful and afraid. *Now* she was fightin' mad! She told her family, "I'm done. I'm seriously done. The devil is *not* going to win this battle!"

She went to her husband's side and said, "Jeff, I'm here."

He turned his head and tried to open his eyes.

"He's in there. He's in there!" she said, and she was flooded with peace.

Things happened quickly. A nurse asked, "Can you raise your eyebrow?"

He did.

Questions came faster. "Wiggle your toes? Squeeze my hand?"

Jeff kept responding.

"Wink one eye? Lift your arm?"

Now he was starting to show off. At one point the man who'd been pretty much declared brain dead gave two thumbs-up.

All through the night and into the morning, family and friends took turns filing in every few hours to watch in amazement as he continued to respond to prompts from the nursing staff.

Later in the morning his neurologist told Erica, "We're going to take scans and see what kind of brain damage he has."

She answered, "I understand you need to run those tests, Doctor, but I want you to know that God's in control and my husband is fine."

Don was supposed to have Thursday off. Instead he asked to come in to work. This was going to be a big day for Jeff, and he wanted to be there.

Jeff was scheduled for CT brain scans, so he'd have to be taken off the ventilator. Don would force air into his lungs by manually squeezing a bag. But he was shocked when, off the ventilator, Jeff was breathing on his own.

That night the scans came back completely normal. Jeff had no brain damage whatsoever.

By Saturday he was sitting in a recliner, eating ice chips and Jell-O.

He went home March 2, just over two weeks after his heart stopped. A pacemaker/defibrillator went with him, and his only residual issue is the need to take a daily supplement for kidneys that no longer retain magnesium.

But the residual blessings . . . ah, that's another story.

As Erica continued to post updates, reports flooded in from families and individuals whose faith had been revitalized through Jeff's ordeal. Moms and dads watched their kids' faith grow after they prayed and then read subsequent posts announcing God's intervention. People of all ages were saying, "I helped pray about that and God answered!"

As stories emerged from all over the nation, Erica, Aubrey, Emily, and Haley began to turn their focus from what God was doing for Jeff to what he was doing for *other* people *through* Jeff.

Not that they've had to look very far.

Don's a regular at Life Church now and has become a good friend of the Buchanans. He says he knows that God still does miracles and that Jeff's not the only one whose life got jump-started.

24

NOTHING TOO DIFFICULT

*When Tim Nowak's brain tumor mysteriously
disappeared, his father knew why.*

One of Tim Nowak's favorite clothing items is a black
T-shirt that says, "I Am Second." It's his way of letting people know God is in charge of his life. His
dad, Dave, well remembers the events that helped them both
realize the truth of those words.

In 2001 the Nowak family lived in the Fort Worth suburb of
Burleson, Texas. Dave served in full-time ministry as a church
co-pastor, jail system chaplain, and founder of a program
for just-released inmates. His wife, Rhonda, was in full-time
ministry too: She homeschooled their four boys.

Seven-year-old Tim was third in the line of brothers. Thin,
blond, quieter than his siblings, he loved to escape the heat
by swimming in the family's backyard pool. That's exactly
what he and two friends were doing, and having a blast,

the afternoon before Independence Day. He wore a plastic "water wing" float with blue and green fish on each arm as he jumped and splashed.

But then he crawled out of the pool and said to his mom, "I feel sick. I think I'm going to throw up." Though he never actually vomited, he did take it easy the rest of the day.

———∞∞———

The next morning Dave noticed him wobbling a bit as he walked. "Tim, you feeling okay?" he asked.

"I don't know, Daddy."

Concerned, Dave called the family doctor, who said Tim had probably swallowed too much water and picked up a bug.

Early that evening the Nowaks were ready to head out to a fireworks display, but Tim still wasn't feeling better. Dave called again.

"You'd better get him over to Cook Children's Hospital," said the doctor.

Thirty minutes later they sat in a Fort Worth emergency room, watching nurses connect Tim to machines. They discovered that the left side of his body wasn't working properly. He couldn't touch his nose with a left-hand finger, couldn't walk a straight line, and seemed disoriented. The staff thought he'd suffered a stroke. After a CT scan, a doctor motioned Dave from the room.

"I'm going to shoot straight with you," he said. "Tim has a tumor the size of an egg on his brain stem."

Only a short time before, Dave had been expecting to spend his evening celebrating with his family. He couldn't believe what he was hearing.

"Are you *sure*?" he asked.

"I've looked at this several times and had a radiologist look at it," the doctor answered. "This is what we believe caused the stroke. We want to admit him tonight and do an MRI in the morning." He explained that the results would help surgeons who wanted to do a biopsy. They needed to find out if the tumor was benign or malignant.

Dave fought to control his rising fear. "Don't sugarcoat it," he said. "What are Tim's options? What's the worst that could happen here?"

"Well, it's not good." He spoke now in a hushed tone. "They might not be able to remove the tumor. He could die. Or he could be a vegetable for the rest of his life. We just don't know until we get in there."

Dave thought about his son lying in a bed on the other side of the door, scared and wondering what was wrong with him. *This can't be happening,* he thought. *It can't be happening. He's going to be all right.*

When a counselor came and explained the situation to the rest of the family, Rhonda broke down, but Dave held his emotions in check. *I've got to be strong. I can't let my wife see me cry. I can't let my boys see me cry.*

Rhonda stayed. Dave drove his other sons home. "Dad, is Tim going to be okay?" one asked.

"Tim will be fine," he said. "He's in God's hands."

He put the boys to bed and walked downstairs to his own room at nearly 2:00 AM. He'd kept himself together throughout the traumatic evening but could hold back no longer. The emotion that burst through the dam was rage.

"God, I'm doing all this stuff for you!" he yelled. "I'm serving people to the point of exhaustion. I'm serving *you.* How can you let this happen to my son? How can you do this to me? Why? *Why?*"

He ranted at the heavens for three hours before collapsing on the bed.

In three more hours Dave was awake again. He dressed, made himself coffee, and sat at the kitchen table. Calmer now, he again turned to God.

"You've heard from me," he prayed. "Now I need to hear from you."

He pulled an old Bible off a bookshelf, the same one he'd received when he'd committed his life to God twelve years before. He intended to read from the Psalms, yet as he laid the Bible on the table, it opened to Jeremiah. He noticed 32:27 underlined in green, but he didn't remember ever marking it.

"Behold, I am the Lord, I am the God over all flesh; is anything too difficult for Me?" (NASB).

Dave stared at the words. *God is speaking to me,* he thought. *It's a question of my faith. Do I believe this is too difficult for him?*

He shut his Bible. "No!" he said aloud.

A strange sensation washed over him. His worries evaporated, replaced by feelings of confidence and peace.

In that instant he understood that Tim would be okay.

———

Later that morning Dave waited at the hospital for Tim and Rhonda to return from the MRI. When they got back to the room, Tim was groggy, with his eyes closed. Dave touched his arm. When Tim opened his eyes, Dave gave him a thumbs-up. Tim smiled for a moment, then went back to sleep.

Rhonda just looked weary.

"How are you doing?" Dave asked his wife.

She managed a worried smile. "I didn't sleep last night."

"It's going to be okay. I've had assurance from God. Everything's going to be all right."

A nurse with short gray hair entered the room and picked up Tim's chart. She frowned as she read. "I saw it. It was there last night," she muttered, more to the chart than to them. "I was here last night when Tim was admitted."

"What are you talking about?" Dave asked.

She looked up. "Has the doctor been in yet?"

"No."

"Well, he'll tell you what's going on." She left without another word.

I already know what's going on, he thought. He suppressed a smile.

Soon the neurologist, a tall man with light brown hair and wire-rimmed glasses, arrived. "Tim has had a stroke on his left side," he said. "We need to find out what caused it."

"What about the egg-sized tumor on his brain stem that the CT scan showed a few hours ago?" Dave asked.

"The MRI did not show a tumor," the physician replied. "So we want to find out what caused the stroke."

Dave was feeling better by the second. "What if the tumor that *was* there—that is no longer there—caused the stroke?"

Silence.

"Doctor, do you believe in miracles? Do you believe in God?"

Again, silence. Then he briefly shook his head. "You need to prepare for Tim to be in rehab for about six months to learn how to walk and talk all over again, because of the severity of the stroke. We'll set up a plan for the rehab. And we're going to do a battery of tests to find out what caused this stroke."

Three days later, during an electrocardiogram, another doctor turned to Dave. "I want you to know that I believe in God," she said. "I've looked at Tim's records, and this is a miracle. You're going to find resistance from the other doctors. They don't believe. They're trying to find something wrong."

After rapid improvement and Tim's sixth day there, the doctors gave up. They sent him home. At a checkup the following week, the neurologist admitted, "I can't explain this. I can't find anything wrong with Tim."

⎯⎯∞⎯⎯

The Nowaks resumed normal life. Several months later they moved to Newcastle, Wyoming, so Dave could pursue a new ministry opportunity. They had lived there about a month when Tim played a football game with his new friends. The next day he complained of pain behind his right ear.

To be safe, Dave drove him to a doctor who turned out to be a Christian. Dave handed him forty pages of records detailing their experience in Texas.

After an exam—and after reading through the medical evidence—the doctor found no sign of problems with Tim. The records of his tumor, he said, indicated nothing short of a miracle.

Though tests were unnecessary, he offered to do a CT scan to try out a new machine. Tim and Dave agreed.

A few days later the doctor called with results. "The scan is negative," he reported. "Tim is fine. But I want you to know that the radiologist did not know of Tim's past medical history. He said he found what looked like scar tissue on Tim's brain stem. It was in the exact spot where the tumor was."

The call simply confirmed what Dave already knew in his heart. The tumor had been there. God had taken it out. It *was* a miracle—though in a way, he figured, it was just God doing what he said he'd do.

⎯⎯∞⎯⎯

Today Dave thinks often of Tim's amazing healing. "Anytime I face a challenge or difficulty, it's something I fall back on," he says. "Nothing is too difficult for God."

Tim, meanwhile, is a healthy seventeen-year-old—tall, still thin, still quiet, with a dream to play college baseball and an aptitude for numbers that appeared only after his hospital stay. He's also thankful to God for the life he's been given.

When people ask what the words on his favorite T-shirt are about, he's always ready to answer: "God is first, and I am second."

25

"FROM SOMEONE WHO CARES"

*An empty pantry and a heartfelt prayer taught
Kelly Knauss a lesson in miracles.*

In the spring of 1997, Kelly Knauss stood in the kitchen of the house he shared with two other college students in Chattanooga, Tennessee. He had the place to himself this morning, which wasn't unusual, since his roommates were often away for days at a time.

He reached into the cupboard and took down a dinner plate and a drinking glass. He set them on the table in front of the chair where he usually sat to eat. From a drawer, he took a single setting of silverware—knife, fork, and spoon—and arranged them neatly on a napkin beside the plate. All set.

Except for one thing. He had no food and no money. His stomach growled to punctuate the real possibility that he might not eat at all that day.

———— ⚭ ————

Just twenty-one at the time, Kelly had never experienced anything like this before. In fact, only a year earlier it looked as if he might never have to think about money again.

He'd become a believer when he was fourteen and then got serious about his faith at seventeen. He felt drawn to a life of full-time ministry and enrolled in a prominent Chicago Bible college. But after flunking out his first year, and suffering through a painful breakup with the girl he thought he'd marry, he wasn't so sure about his future in the church.

"I was disappointed by how things were turning out," he recalled. "I wandered away from God and questioned everything I felt certain of before."

Disheartened, he flew home to Chattanooga—and promptly landed in the lap of luxury. He went to work for the owners of a pest control business and began dating their daughter. They welcomed him as if he were already family and began grooming him to move up the company ladder quickly. The girl's father showered him with unexpected "pocket money" and expensive gifts.

"My birthday present that year was a trip to the Bahamas," he said. "Suddenly I had money to throw around, and I started thinking, *I can chase this dream. I can make this my life.* But deep down I knew it wasn't right. Even though the money was alluring, I was already feeling discontent with that lifestyle."

Eventually Kelly's dissatisfaction led to a moment of decision. One day he found himself crawling through sewage under a house with leaking pipes. He was there to assess termite damage, which almost certainly was not as bad as he would have to make it sound to sell the owner a treatment package. Suddenly, in that cramped, dank crawl space, he saw himself clearly following in the footsteps of the prodigal son—running from God and from the life he was meant to lead. Not long after, he broke up with the girl and said good-bye to her family. He took a month-long road trip to Colorado, trying to gain clarity and get back on track. Once home, he enrolled part time at a local college.

At first, money still was not a problem. He liked to buy and sell sports cars, and he worked on commission for a friend who owned a nearby lot. He was a natural salesman and never lacked for anything.

"Being a single guy in my early twenties, I tried to live extravagantly, owning three nice sports cars and a motor-cycle," he said. "My friends described me as free-spirited, independent, and wealthy for my age. I certainly wanted to appear that way."

About that time, a friend asked Kelly to consider join-ing a youth ministry called Student Venture, run by Campus Crusade for Christ. While the idea of working with teens intrigued him, there was a major problem with the plan: As a Campus Crusade member, he'd have to raise his own support. The thought of being completely dependent on the generosity of donors held little appeal for him. His friend persisted, though, and Kelly promised to at least pray about it.

Then things began to change.

"God's answer when I prayed was always the same—that I should trust in *him* to provide instead of putting trust in myself or a steady paycheck. Yet at the same time, I felt that he pulled the rug out from under my feet."

Now the cars Kelly bought, hoping to turn them around for quick profit, wouldn't sell. His healthy income quickly looked anemic. Desperate, he got a job cleaning a church, just two doors down from his house, but had to wait nearly a month for work to begin. In other words, he was broke. *Really* broke.

Kelly looked at the place setting he'd just laid out. He knew there was no food in the house and no money in his wallet. But he'd once heard the story of a Prussian minister named George Müller who cared for many thousands of orphans in Bristol, England, in the mid-nineteenth century. Müller never asked for financial assistance and never went into debt. Yet the needs of his five orphanages were always met, often at precisely the critical moment.

One morning the kitchen staff informed Müller there was nothing for the children to eat for breakfast that day. He instructed them to set the tables as usual. When the children sat down, he gave thanks for the food as he always did. Just then there was a knock at the door: A neighborhood baker had arrived with enough bread to feed everyone, followed by a milkman whose loaded cart had broken down just in front of the orphanage. God had provided at the very moment Müller and his hungry orphans needed him to.

"I'm no George Müller," Kelly said. "But I asked God to provide my dinner that night, in spite of the fact that I was full of doubt. *What if I ask and God doesn't answer? What if his answer is no? What if I didn't pray hard enough?* But I also had to see what would happen *if* God said yes."

He admits it wouldn't have been the first time God answered a similar prayer. Only recently he'd asked for side work he could do while waiting for his new job to start. A man who lived nearby knocked within minutes and said, "Do you happen to know of anyone looking for side work? I need help with a bunch of odd jobs." That had led to a week's wages.

But asking for food to appear out of thin air seemed different somehow.

Kelly left the house and walked to the church where he'd soon be working full time. That day he'd agreed to help the regular maintenance man, Roger, with a project or two. Several hours later, the work was done and he was ready to head home. Determined to follow Müller's example, he'd said nothing of his need.

Roger stopped him before he could leave and said, "Hey, Kelly, do you want any of the food in the benevolence pantry?" He explained that much of it had reached its expiration date and would have to be thrown out if no one used it.

"Of course, I was thinking of the empty dishes I'd set out on my table at home, so I told him I could use a box of cereal. He gave me one, but then just kept pulling things out of the closet. By the time he was done, I had a box of dried and canned goods that must have weighed eighty pounds. I could barely carry it. And I was amazed what God had just done."

Afraid the bottom would fall out before he could get it home, Kelly set it on the sidewalk outside and went to get his car. Then, when he arrived back at his front door, he was astonished to find three full grocery bags leaning against it with a note attached: *From someone who cares.*

Stunned, he retrieved the box and carried it inside. When he went to collect the bags, a car pulled into the driveway. Trish, a woman from the church, leaned out the window. "I was at the store and God put it in my heart to bring you some food," she called. Then she got out and handed him three grocery bags full of frozen goods.

She drove away and he went inside, barely able to contain his excitement and gratitude. God had answered, and then some! He would eat tonight; more than that, he felt revived in his faith, knowing his needs would be met.

"I felt like God was right there in the room with me," he said. "I laid out the groceries on the counter, but soon it was completely full. So I put food on the table, but then that filled up also. I had to put the rest on the kitchen floor."

It was enough food for eight weeks. And it was sufficient evidence of God's provision to convince Kelly to call his friend and take the position with Student Venture.

"God can provide if we trust him," said Kelly, who now serves as a pastor in Wisconsin. "Since then, when things seem difficult, I just remember the time I asked God for one meal and he fed me for two months."

26

"Rise Up"

Unaware of her life-threatening disease, Rosanne Marshall acted because of divine direction. Just in time.

On a cold morning on the last day of October 2006, Rosanne Marshall was dozing in bed when she heard a voice.

"Wake up. Rise up. Rise up!"

She opened her eyes and looked around, expecting to see her husband. The room was empty. It couldn't have been Joe's voice—he'd already left for work. Besides, she couldn't imagine him using an expression like "rise up."

She looked at the clock: 6:43 AM. Her kids weren't up yet. Obviously she'd been dreaming.

She closed her eyes again and went back to dozing.

And she heard it again.

"Rise up."

She opened her eyes.

The words she heard next filled her with fear: "You have cancer. Time is important. I will give you unbelievable peace. I will be with you."

Rosanne's fear really did give way to peace—a huge wave of peace that enveloped her completely. She lay there a moment, letting everything soak in. She'd just heard an audible voice. That had never, ever happened to her before. Strangely, though, the voice was not unfamiliar.

Now what?

She got up and reached for the phone. Her OB/GYN, located in her home city of Atlanta, kept earlier office hours than her family doctor so she'd try there first, but basically she'd go to whomever she could reach first. She gave the receptionist her name and asked for an appointment.

"What is the reason for the appointment?"

She didn't quite know how to answer, so she blurted, "My yearly exam."

The receptionist had pulled up her records by then. "You aren't due yet for your annual. Are you having any symptoms?"

"No, but I need to see someone anyway," she hedged, not ready to explain about the voice.

"Tell me what you're experiencing," the woman prodded, puzzled.

Suddenly Rosanne burst into tears. "I think something's wrong and I need to see someone."

The office got her in the following day. As the doctor neared the end of the exam, she said, "Nothing seems out of order. Everything seems fine."

Rosanne prayed, *God, you're going to have to show me what to do here.*

The physician pressed on her stomach. Suddenly she yelped in pain.

"How long has that been going on?"

"It hasn't."

An ultrasound revealed a marble-sized cyst on an ovary. The doctor said, "We'll keep an eye on that" and sent her home.

Again she prayed, *God, you're going to have to show me what to do.*

———⚭———

Two weeks later Rosanne kept an appointment for minor surgery to repair complications from the birth of her third baby, now two. While she was there, the doctor did a colonoscopy and then delivered a strange report: "Your appendix looked odd," he said. "There was some mucus and we did a biopsy, and everything is fine but I just wanted to tell you about it."

In another week she felt so bad she couldn't get out of bed. Along with a bloated stomach, she had such severe fatigue she cancelled the neighborhood Christmas party that was to take place at her house.

She went to her OB/GYN for another ultrasound. The technician said the doctor, on vacation, would take a look at it when she returned in January.

"I don't want to wait until January," Rosanne protested. "I feel horrible."

The tech thought a moment, then said, "I'll email the results to the doctor, and if she's concerned she'll call you."

"Can you tell me if the cyst has grown?" Rosanne asked.

"I can't tell you that."

"Okay, is it still the size of a marble?"

"No. It's not the size of a marble."

The next day the doctor called. When she said she was in the car with her kids, the doctor asked her to pull over.

"Why?"

"I'm calling you on my cell phone from vacation. I don't usually give this information over the phone, but that tiny marble is now the size of a lemon and there are two of them. I need you to call Dr. Linda Pratt, a gynecological oncologist. I think you have full-blown cancer."

On January 9 she saw Dr. Pratt, who looked at her scans and said, "I'm not really worried about this. I don't think this is cancer. We'll get you in for surgery in February or March."

Rosanne looked at her husband, then back at Dr. Pratt. "I don't think you understand," she said firmly. "I'll be dead by March."

The operation took place January 24. It wasn't a benign cyst after all, and the doctor broke the news when she woke: "Rosanne, you have stage-four cancer of the appendix. It spread to your ovaries, and when you came in the tumors had already ruptured—the cancer is throughout your abdomen. I removed your ovaries and fallopian tubes and did a belly wash. I tried to see where it was coming from, and that's when I saw there was mucus all over your appendix. I did what I could, but you'll have to find a specialist."

Rosanne and Joe decided to pursue treatment at the MD Anderson Center in Houston, which specializes in rare cancers. In addition, Rosanne's brother and his wife live fifteen minutes from the center.

One evening a few weeks later, right before they were scheduled to leave for Houston, they were talking in the den. The house was quiet, the children all asleep, and Joe was thoughtful, pondering what had happened. Doctors had told them that appendix cancer is rare, with few symptoms until it has progressed. As it's rarely discovered early, the prognosis usually isn't good.

"Rosanne, if you hadn't been proactive you wouldn't be alive right now. How did you know? You went to the doctor in October when you had no symptoms. I've been wondering, why did you make an appointment then?"

"I'm going to tell you, Joe. God spoke to me. Not through song or words I read in the Bible, but through an audible voice I heard with my ears."

This was the first time she'd told anyone about the voice. She watched for her husband's reaction. He was listening intensely to her every word.

She continued, "I'd heard of God speaking to people, but I never thought it would happen to me. Sometimes you wonder, *If God spoke to me like that, what would I do? Would I dismiss it? Would I listen?* But Joe, it was so strong I couldn't dismiss it. Plus, there was something familiar about the voice, and it really did give me comfort and peace that passed all understanding. So I believed. I didn't know if people around me were ready to believe, so I kept it quiet, just a private thing between God and me. But I knew I'd be ready to talk about it when the time was right."

Joe held her hands, and she knew that he believed as well.

Now it was time to find out if anyone else would believe what Rosanne had experienced. The next opportunity to tell her story came a week later in Houston as she met with the surgeons and doctors who would be treating her cancer. They were so amazed at her timing of seeking help that they asked to interview her for a book on rare cancers to be published by Harvard. And that's how she found herself answering questions in a crowded room filled with surgeons, oncologists, interns, and other medical staff.

Her surgeon said, "Rosanne, you're very young. People we see with this cancer usually are in their fifties, with no symptoms, and it's too late for them by the time they get to us. You're different. You're thirty-nine. And you're here sooner. How did you know? What made you get help?"

She took a deep breath. "Actually, God spoke to me."

"What do you mean?"

"God spoke to me in an audible voice. He told me I had cancer, time was important, and that he would see me through."

The room fell silent.

After a moment he said, "Well, that's about the only thing you could have told me that made sense. You'll make it, Rosanne. You have faith. You listen. And you believe."

The next step would be a fourteen-hour procedure in which her surgeons would open her up, remove every one of her organs, peel the cancer off, sew each organ back in, then pour in a container of heated chemotherapy chemicals everywhere, and let her sit for two hours before sewing her back up. Then she would remain in the hospital a month.

They scheduled surgery for April 11. In the meantime she returned home. She still had peace, though sometimes she got discouraged too.

One day Rosanne was feeling extremely low but went to pick up a book for a friend. While she was waiting in line, a man entered the store. In his mid-fifties, he was wearing dirty clothes and boots. He walked to the corner of the sales counter and started talking to a clerk.

The woman in front of Rosanne was taking a long time with several returns, so she had plenty of time to observe the man. Since he was talking in a normal voice just a few feet away, she'd also overheard his conversation.

They were speaking about someone who had worked at this bookstore. "Nice guy," he said. "I heard he got married."

The clerk nodded. "Yeah, he and his new wife live on the other side of town now."

"Well, I know his family. Wonderful Christian family. Did you know that when he was a kid—I think about five—he was diagnosed with spinal meningitis and had brain damage?"

Rosanne was watching the man's eyes—the clearest, bluest eyes she'd ever seen.

"In fact, doctors told his folks he had brain damage and would never be anything but a vegetable if he even lived until morning. So they went home that night, and they were praying, and his dad heard God speak in an audible voice: 'I've heard your prayers and answered them. Go see your son.'

"The father went to the hospital at 3:00 AM, and his son was still completely unresponsive. So he prayed and said, 'God, you told me he's healed, so I'm not going to leave this bedside till I see it.' And in the morning, the boy woke up and said, 'Daddy, where's Mom?' And even the doctors said it was a miracle, that there was absolutely nothing wrong with the boy."

Rosanne was at the counter by now. She paid for her things. Heading toward the exit, she passed the man and said, "Thank you for your story."

He looked deep into her eyes. "Ma'am, do you believe God heals people?"

"Yes."

"All you have to do is believe."

"I believe," she told him. "I really do believe!"

Rosanne's doctors said her surgery was one of the most successful they had ever done. Tumors reappeared a year later, so they performed it a second time.

Today she is cancer-free.

Recently she was getting her hair done in a local salon when someone asked how she was feeling. She talked about how the cancer had returned but now was gone.

Suddenly a customer in an adjacent station turned to her. "Excuse me, you said you had cancer?"

"Yes."

"Can I ask your name?"

Rosanne told her.

The woman started crying. "Someone in my prayer group heard about your story back when you first got sick, and we've been praying for you ever since! I never thought I'd get to meet you."

Reflecting on her experiences, Rosanne says she doesn't know why God spoke to her the way he did, when he doesn't speak to everyone in the same way. She doesn't know why she was blessed with the prayers of so many, even strangers. She says, "We don't carry the burden to understand it. That's God's burden. Our job is to trust and stay faithful."

She adds, "When God heals you, you don't know if it'll be immediately, over time, or through medical treatment. It might even be through death, since heaven will bring total healing and wholeness. I do know that God loves us, and that if we keep on trusting him through adversity he'll take care of us. All we have to do is believe in God's power and provision."

27

A MATTER OF LIFE OR DEATH

During the birth of her son, Mary Towns found herself
transformed in ways she would never have imagined.

Mary Towns had waited long enough. She was ready
to have this baby!

It was the morning of December 2, 1981. Mary
was a nurse in St. Louis, pregnant with her first child. She'd
learned via an ultrasound it was a boy. For what seemed like
forever, she and her husband, Tom, had looked forward to
the birth of their son.

But then the due date came and went. Now she was at the
hospital, three weeks overdue. She suffered from what quickly
would be diagnosed as toxemia, including swelling from ex-
cessive fluid. She had difficulty breathing. She'd been in labor
with almost no medication nearly twenty-eight hours—one
for each year of her life.

At this point the number in both cases felt closer to a hundred.

To complicate matters further, the baby was "sunny side up," or face forward. The result was intense back pain with each contraction. It all added up to the most agony she'd ever endured.

As the clock in her room approached 11:00 AM, Mary was finally almost fully dilated. Then a nurse brought the discouraging news that the doctor was performing an emergency caesarean section and wasn't available yet. She had to wait on her back, every contraction excruciating.

Mary was a woman of faith with an active prayer life. Too exhausted and hurting to form sentences or even thoughts, she uttered wordless prayers. God would understand.

Growing up in a home plagued by alcoholism, emotional abuse, and divorce had left her struggling with feelings of shame, worthlessness, and anxiety. She trusted God to help her yet also felt tied to the world and its problems. She feared a variety of illnesses and death. On this day in particular, she was keenly aware of all that can go wrong during childbirth.

She focused on the tiny dots on the ceiling tiles as she fought. Her body, and her faith, felt so feeble.

Suddenly the ceiling rippled and appeared to open. Incredibly she saw Jesus, arms outstretched on the cross, clouds and sky behind him. In a similar position on the bed, Mary felt herself slowly rising to meet him. She ascended until they were face-to-face—then kept rising until they'd somehow merged.

She'd never experienced anything like it. Her spirit was one with Jesus' spirit. Filled with profound peace, she felt deeply and personally loved by God. Overwhelmed, tears of joy ran down her face.

A voice interrupted, and instantly she was back in the bed. "Your doctor is out of the operating room," an anesthesiologist said. "We're ready for you!"

Mary felt grief-stricken over the sudden loss of joy and peace. The staff sat her up to administer anesthesia, and her water broke. She felt disconnected from the earth, with no sense of gravity. "Don't let me fall, Jesus!" she cried. "Don't let me fall!"

Strong arms hoisted her onto a stretcher. Hospital staff rushed her down the hall to a delivery room, where she was placed on a table. Nurses lifted her legs into stirrups. The doctor arrived and lifted the blue drape covering her.

"Oh my God!" he said. "I've got a prolapsed umbilical cord here. I'm losing the pulse in the cord!"

He's in trouble, Mary thought. *My baby is in serious trouble.* She knew that when the cord comes out first, the baby is cut off from its life-giving flow of oxygen and nutrients. It was too late for surgery—he'd already started to emerge. Her son had to be delivered in the next three minutes or he would die.

The overhead clock read 11:15.

The surrounding team went into action. The doctor made an incision to create more room for the baby's exit. They enlisted Tom and a nurse to help push on her abdomen while the doctor pulled at the baby's head with forceps.

She checked the clock: 11:16.

She held her breath. *Is he going to make it? Is he going to make it?*

11:17.

She heard the sickening crunch of breaking bone.

"That was either your tailbone or the baby's collarbone," the doctor said.

The anesthesiologist monitoring her vital signs said quietly, "I don't have a blood pressure here."

Then Mary felt a dramatic release. Her head began to swim.

Instantly, unaccountably, she separated from her physical self. She was spirit only, on the ceiling, looking down on the room. She saw a large puddle of red on and around the doctor's feet. She saw the terrified look on Tom's face. She saw her new baby lying on her own stomach, blue and limp.

She felt a crushing sadness. She didn't know for certain if her son was dead, but she feared the worst. *If I've just labored twenty-eight hours for a dead baby,* she thought, *I may as well die too.*

Her spirit turned away from the scene below and toward a brilliant light above. She yearned for the sense of contentment and love she'd experienced just a few minutes before. She wanted to go back to what had felt like home.

In this state, truths that had been unattainable before now became clear. Mary realized she was an eternal, spiritual being, made for relationship with God. Shame and fear melted away. She recognized her body as a temporary covering, what the Bible describes as a "tent."

As she processed this startling knowledge, a silent question emerged in her mind: *Will you return?*

In that moment she was filled with a hunger to find out if her son had survived. She *had* to know. Without speaking, she answered, *Yes, Lord.*

Immediately she was back in her body on the table. She labored to breathe and felt her heart surge into action again. She opened her eyes to the beautiful sight of her newborn, struggling to lift his head from her abdomen.

For an instant the head rose. His open eyes locked on to hers.

Mary sensed a powerful, spiritual link. It seemed her son was the only one in the room who knew she had "left."

Satisfied that his mother had returned, the baby laid his head back down and sighed.

With shaky hands the proud father cut his son's umbilical cord. The doctor picked the baby up and examined him. "He has good muscle tone now," he said. "His second Apgar score is going to be nine. That's very good considering where he was when he first came out. That broken collarbone is a small price to pay to be alive."

Mary, overcome with relief, turned and said, "I'm sorry about all the blood on your shoes."

He raised his eyebrows. From her position she couldn't possibly see his shoes.

Mary has no doubt she experienced two miracles that day. The first was the twin delivery room encounters; the second was when she easily might have slipped away into death. She now feels completely loved by God and transformed in her faith. She has lost her fear of dying and is far less plagued by everyday concerns. She embraces these words: "God has not given us a spirit of fear, but of power and of love and of a sound mind" (2 Timothy 1:7).

Some ask her how she knows her encounters weren't hallucinations, dreams, or chemical reactions to trauma. "I have experienced all those things before or since that day," she answers. "None of those experiences had any positive or lasting effect. This is an experience that changed me for life."

Mary changed so much that she took up pastoral counseling. Today she's a nurse practitioner in Salt Lake City and is on the staff of Roi House of Prayer, a facility where anyone of faith can gather to worship and pray.

The other miracle from that day in St. Louis is the life of her son. Thomas Towns, the baby who almost didn't survive his birth, has grown into a man of courage and compassion, a person who has touched many lives through his care for the disabled and for those suffering from cancer.

He now works, as an operating room technician, at the same hospital as his mother in Salt Lake City.

28

No Explanation

Megan Conner's X-rays showed as many as eighteen back fractures. So why did the MRI show nothing wrong?

At eleven years old, Megan Conner had everything going for her. She was a good student, organized, witty, and popular with her friends. She was growing up in sunny Southern California, where she could regularly play soccer, a sport she loved. She had an older sister and two younger brothers to enjoy. She was the daughter of a devoted mother and a father who served God as a pastor.

But as the saying goes, there was trouble in paradise.

The first hints that her idyllic world was about to crumble occurred in December 2008. She began to forget things. One day she walked into her classroom and couldn't remember where to sit. In the following weeks she dissolved into crying fits. She insulted the boys in the school band, not at all her typical behavior. She grew panicky and withdrawn.

Early in 2009, her parents, Jim and Lynda, took her to an emergency room for tests. A neurologist said she was fine physically and referred her to a counselor. But ten days later they received a middle-of-the-night call from a youth leader. Megan, on a church youth retreat, had suffered a grand mal seizure. She'd bitten her tongue until it bled and temporarily lost consciousness.

Lynda drove through a stormy night to pick up Megan. After they went to an ER, they got back on an LA freeway to head home. However, in the car, Megan seemed lethargic. Suddenly she began shaking. She bit her tongue again. Her mouth bled and foamed.

Lynda, horrified and panicked, pulled off and called Jim.

"She's having a seizure!" she cried. "What should I do? I can't get through on 9-1-1! I don't know what to do!"

Jim calmed his wife enough to help her find another ER, where doctors medicated and stabilized Megan. The following weeks were marked by more scares, more hospital visits, more tests, a new neurologist, and more questions. Gradually Megan declined until she lapsed into a mostly catatonic state.

Finally the Conners received a diagnosis. Megan had systemic lupus erythematosus, an autoimmune disease that can lead to a host of lifelong complications, one in which antibodies mistakenly attack healthy tissue—in Megan's case, her brain. Untreated, SLE could be lethal.

There was no cure.

They listened in shock and wept as doctors explained what lay ahead: aggressive treatment, including steroids and chemotherapy; weight gain; hair loss; missing one to three years of school; special tutors; a speech therapist; having to stay out of the sun; and the chance of sterilization.

No parents want to see their child suffer. Jim just wished he could trade places with his daughter. How, he wondered, could all of this be happening?

—————ꝏ—————

However, Megan's family did have a "secret weapon" for fighting back: prayer. Jim asked God what they should pray for. He sensed the answer was to ask that Megan wake up from her coma-like condition. His church had a prayer chain of believers, so he made that single request and soon was amazed to find people praying for Megan in the hospital lobby. He found out they also prayed for his strength. He felt the result of their efforts—the "peace of Christ that passes all understanding." It was a ray of hope in the midst of dark times.

After enduring terrifying hallucinations, Megan did slowly wake up, still frightened and confused. She couldn't speak but was able to communicate via text messages. After twelve days in the hospital, she was given a hefty supply of medications and allowed to go home.

That first day she bawled because she gagged on her pills. She couldn't swallow them. She felt panicked. How would she make it if she couldn't even take her medicine?

Jim again prayed about the problem. "God," he said, "what do you want us to do about this?" He felt led to ask the prayer chain to pray that his daughter would be able to take her medication.

For Megan, the next day was indeed a different story.

"I just swallowed my pills!" she told her parents, excited. "It was easy. It didn't bother me at all." These were her first complete sentences in weeks.

She continued to take her medications and applied sunscreen all over her body daily to ward off the lupus-triggering effects of sunlight. She had good and bad days. Her hair fell out and she gained considerable weight due to the steroids. Kids teased her at school. By June she also complained of back pain.

Yet she felt strong enough to accompany her family (minus Jim, preaching in Egypt) and her aunt's family, including eight kids, to a vacation in the San Bernardino Mountains. They all ventured to an outdoor water park, and despite the discomfort in her back, Megan begged to go down the twisting, three-hundred-foot-long waterslide.

"I don't know, honey," Lynda said.

"I want to try," Megan prodded. "I'll be okay. I don't want to just sit in the shade and do nothing."

Lynda relented.

A few minutes later she regretted her decision. Megan came off the slide in tears. The pain was so intense that she cried for the next ninety minutes.

At the next checkup, Lynda mentioned Megan's complaints. The doctor ordered a CT scan. When he looked at the results, he saw as many as eighteen fractures. He asked Lynda to step into the hallway with him.

"This is bad," he said. "You should have told me sooner. The scan shows multiple fractures. The steroids have stolen all the calcium; this looks like the spine of a sixty- or seventy-year-old woman with advanced osteoporosis."

Lynda drew in a breath. "What can we do about it?"

"There's nothing we *can* do," he answered. "This is permanent. This is how Megan's going to be for the rest of her life."

For Megan and her parents, this came as yet another terrible blow.

Later that week Jim was in Room 12, a classroom at church, with a few staff members. Sunlight shone brightly through glass windows, but the beautiful weather didn't match his feelings. He grieved for his daughter and the lifelong hardships she faced.

He related the bad news about Megan's back. Then he bowed his head to pray: "What do you want us to do, God? How do you want us to pray?"

During the past difficult months, every time he'd asked for guidance about what to pray for, the answer had been for resolution to whatever specific problem they faced. But this time he heard these words in his mind: *I can heal her.* At the same time he saw a picture of Megan's spine. It was perfectly straight and strong.

Yet he resisted. *I don't want to pray, God. I don't want to be disappointed. I don't want to be wrong.* Still the impression remained.

He told the staff. The word went out to the prayer chain. They would ask for healing of Megan's back.

───⦿───

Megan's doctor had ordered an MRI to show the extent of the damage. The next day, July 7, at her chemotherapy appointment, the doctor said, "I'm sorry I don't have the MRI results for you yet. I need to ask for them again. There's something wrong with the report from the technician."

Soon afterward he called and spoke with Lynda.

"Mrs. Conner," he said, "I'm sorry, I got the same MRI report again. Could you go down there and pick up the physical DVD and films and bring them to me at Megan's next appointment so I can see them?"

She did just that. Meanwhile, Megan stopped complaining of back pain.

The Conners soon met with the doctor. He had examined the images, and he spoke to them with a bewildered look.

"Look, I've got these MRI results," he said. He seemed to be searching for the right words. "I asked for them because I couldn't figure out what was wrong. I thought they'd sent me the wrong results.

"I've got a CT scan that shows all of these back fractures," he continued. "And I have an MRI that shows she's fine. There is no medical explanation for that. I don't know what to tell you about what happened."

Megan and her parents looked at each other and smiled. They had a pretty good idea.

───❧───

Megan is not completely free of the effects of lupus—at least, not yet. She has almost no memory of the second half of 2008, and she battles short-term memory loss. Memorization in high school classes like math and languages is a challenge. She still covers herself with sunblock every day.

Yet she's earning A's through old-fashioned hard work and discipline. She's played another season of soccer. She never needed special tutors or a speech therapist. In fact, her speaking ability rebounded so well that she earned a third-place trophy for dramatic interpretation in a competitive speech and debate tournament.

More important, her health has rebounded as well. Since her amazing healing, she's had no back troubles at all. She's off steroids and is taking only a single maintenance drug. Her doctor recently told her relieved father, "The only word I can use for your daughter is *cured*."

"I don't know what you call that," Jim said, "but I call it a miracle."

29

"TONIGHT I'M GOING TO TAKE YOU TO HEAVEN"

*Grieving the loss of his son, Trevor Yaxley
didn't have to die for a visit.*

A few days before Christmas 1986, the residents of northern New Zealand got what they'd been praying for—an end to the punishing drought that had left the island's normally verdant landscape parched and brown.

But they didn't expect the first rain in months to arrive on the powerful and destructive winds of Cyclone Raja, currently making its way northward in the Pacific toward Fiji.

On the evening the storm arrived, Trevor and Jan Yaxley had just finished leading an evangelical rally for several hundred local teenagers at a meeting hall not far from their home. Darkness had fallen by the time they left the building and headed into the torrential rain and lashing wind. They were soaked the moment they stepped out the door.

Trevor pulled onto SH 1 for the short drive. He hadn't gone far when a fierce gust pushed the car effortlessly across the pavement into the oncoming lane. He steered back to the proper side and commented to Jan how fortunate they had been that no cars were coming toward them just then.

"It was absolutely blowing a gale," Trevor said. "Really terrible weather and very dangerous driving conditions."

As they carefully made their way through the storm, they thought of their two children who'd left an hour earlier and headed home along the same route. Sixteen-year-old David was driving, his sister, Rebecca, with him. The concerned parents said a prayer—and tried not to worry about the hazardous stretch of road ahead.

The Yaxleys were familiar with highway accidents. As well-known ministers in the area, they often accompanied emergency responders to provide spiritual assistance as needed. Only a week ago they'd been present when a young person died in a terrible wreck. In other words, they knew better than most people what was at stake on a night like this.

"By the time we reached Dome Valley, just a few miles from home, we saw that the road ahead was completely blocked by an accident," Trevor said. "It was a horrendous sight, with flares burning and lights flashing everywhere. A helicopter was trying to land to assist."

There were no other cars ahead of them, and he pulled right up to the police barricade.

"I turned to Jan and said, 'Honey, brace yourself, I think something terrible has happened.' I told her to stay in the car and I would go see."

Jan said, "It's David! It's David! I know it's David!"

Although their daughter was also in the vehicle, their hearts told them that something awful had happened to their son.

As Trevor crossed the barricade and walked into the scene, he saw immediately that the cars involved were "totally wrecked and torn apart." The rain continued to pour, drenching him to the skin, but his only thought was the growing stone-cold awareness that one of the cars belonged to David.

Just then a teenage boy named Andrew, a member of David's youth group who'd been traveling in another car, approached and fell into Trevor's arms, sobbing and unable to speak. His presence confirmed what Trevor suspected. Pain and dread flooded his body. He raised his hands to God.

"Somehow I said to him, 'Though you slay me, yet will I trust you'" (see Job 13:15). "Even at that time I felt God clearly speaking to me. 'You just watch what takes place now, and you will see what I can do in a person's life.'"

Trevor and Jan buried David on Christmas Eve. To attend the funeral, they had to leave thirteen-year-old Rebecca in the hospital's intensive care unit, being treated for injuries from the crash. She eventually recovered.

And life went on. Sort of.

The couple decided to continue their work with Lifeway Ministries, the organization they founded when Trevor left a lucrative career in business to realign priorities to his family and community. The calendar was already packed with speaking engagements and rallies.

But nearly two years after David's death, the pain was still fresh for him. The joy and light had still not returned to his life. They had seen thousands touched by God in their ministry, but his heart was still wounded and raw.

In 1988 the Yaxleys embarked on a trip to the South Island. After twelve days of leading as many as three daily meetings, Trevor and Jan, physically and emotionally exhausted, arrived in the city of Invercargill for the tour's final rally. That night, waiting to begin, Trevor looked out over the packed auditorium. Every seat was filled—except one. It was in the front row, right where David always sat when he accompanied them to meetings like this one.

"David was a very hip kid, very cool," Trevor recalled. "The other kids loved having him around. He was also a Christian leader. He was my chief cheerleader at these engagements. When I saw that empty seat that night, I felt his absence very strongly. Then the devil said to me, 'See, he's gone. Everything will be a shambles. Nothing will happen tonight, because you don't have anything to say.'"

It didn't work. Trevor told Satan to stand aside. And the evening was a tremendous success.

That night Trevor fell into bed worn out, body and soul. He missed David as much as ever. He began to pray. Despite everything he could see the Lord doing through their ministry, he asked God for reassurance that he and Jan were in the right place, doing the right thing.

God answered: *"Yes, you are. And, by the way, tonight I'm going to take you to heaven."*

What was that? He'd learned to trust the sound of God's voice when he spoke in times like this. But had he heard correctly what God was promising?

"Somehow I knew that didn't mean I was going to die," he said. "But I was amazed at the possibility it might really happen. I tried to go to sleep. But when God says he's going to take you to heaven, you can't go to sleep!"

Trevor tossed and turned most of the night.

"At about six o'clock it was still dark outside. I was lying on my back, and I said to God, 'You haven't got much time left, only a couple of hours.' As the words left my mouth, an absolutely incredible thing happened."

Suddenly he felt as if he were flying upward so fast he could barely breathe. He felt pressure on his body, like the wind resistance on a speeding motorcycle—only greater. The tremendous rate of travel made it difficult to open his eyes. He had the impression of moving past many bright lights.

Then he felt an enormous "thump" as his feet landed on solid ground.

"At first I felt really wobbly," he said. "As I opened my eyes, the sights and sounds and scents just flooded my senses. All of them were instantly heightened beyond anything I'd ever experienced. I was especially aware of the most amazing fragrance. It is completely impossible to explain how wonderful it was. You don't just smell it. You *experience* it. It affects your whole body. It affects *you*."

Trevor instantly felt an overwhelming sense of well-being. His body was flooded with an intense feeling of acceptance, love, and understanding.

He looked to his left and beheld an immense, beautiful tree.

"I immediately noticed incredible differences between this tree and the ones we have on earth," he said. "It was emitting its own light. Light didn't shine on things there—it came out of everything. I was surrounded by light."

Trying to cope with his heightened emotions, he noticed he was standing on a path that wound its way downward, away from the tree. Then he sensed someone standing behind him. He turned and saw a person who emitted light in the same way as the tree. Trevor noticed only his radiant face that exuded love and kindness—and that he was speaking without moving his lips. Communication was forming in Trevor's mind without the need for sound.

"Hey, how are you doing?" the man asked, matter-of-factly. "How long have you been here?"

"I told him that I'd just arrived," Trevor said. "But I was stunned, because it was like he was speaking with two voices. Underlying what he'd said was this stream of affirmation that continuously kept telling me what an amazing person I am and what wonderful qualities I have. I will never be able to express the joy I felt at this."

As the person was speaking, Trevor noticed a nearby building that looked like a child's playhouse. The man beckoned him to follow inside. He ducked his head through the low doorway and saw a spacious room filled with equally radiant people.

"As I looked at all these people, I saw an expression come on the face of the one who'd been speaking to me. Everybody looked up at me and smiled. Suddenly I just knew everything had been prearranged. You just know, you don't have to ask. I knew God had set this up for me as a father. I knew my son was behind me. I turned around, and there he was on the path."

Just as he'd done often in life, David smiled at his father and enticed him to play a game of chase. "See if you can catch me!" he called, turning and running down the path past the tree.

"My son looked so full of life!" Trevor said. "This wasn't a dream. It was utterly real."

He didn't want to chase David. He wanted to *hold* him. He excused himself from the people in the playhouse and took off running. He noticed he wasn't expending energy at all as he would have on earth. He didn't grow winded or tired. He felt as if all heaven's energy was *one*, and it was all fused into himself.

"As I was following David, I noticed I was standing on these unbelievable flowers. They were transparent, with incredible

214

colors like you can't imagine—and they were *humming*. I know how crazy that sounds, but they were humming praise to God. Nothing was broken. I felt guilty about even standing on them, but they would just stand straight back up again."

He continued running after David. The path led through a stand of trees where leaves were falling to the ground in a carpet of light. Again he was struck that there was light everywhere, coming from everything. Then he caught up with David, and they embraced.

"I could feel the muscles on his back and could smell him again. The look on his face was one of absolute delight and peace. His eyes were so clear, and he was so pure it was almost scary. There was nothing in him other than purity. He was changed, and yet he was still himself. He was perfect."

David said, "How is Mom's garden going? I'm glad to see you're still growing things."

Just before he died he'd helped Trevor plant a garden in the yard for Jan.

"I said it was doing great, but I didn't want to talk about Mom's garden. I asked him, 'How are *you*?'"

"Wonderful! Let me show you around."

David took his father's hand and led him through a field covered in what looked like "freshly mown velvet." Everything was arranged with a "random perfection." There were houses spread across the field that Trevor knew were waiting to be occupied by God's people. He was overcome by the beauty of what he was seeing and by the joy of being with David. He began to cry.

"Don't cry, Dad," David said tenderly. "Nobody cries here."

"I'm just so happy, I can't help it!"

"But there is no *need* to cry."

As they were speaking, David's voice started to fade, and things felt to Trevor as if they were "going in reverse." He felt himself moving again—backward this time—at incredible speed. He felt his body hit the motel bed where he'd spent the night back on earth. It landed with a jolt and a thump.

He immediately burst into tears. Jan jumped out of bed and ran to his side. For a long time he only sobbed while she comforted him.

"I couldn't talk about my experience to anybody but Jan for a long time," Trevor said. "Everybody told me, 'You're different, what's happened?' But I couldn't tell the story. It was too close. Even so, from that day on I was a totally different man. My grief had gone and my joy had returned. I was able to smile and laugh and play again."

His trip to heaven that night energized his desire to tell others about God's grace and salvation—something he and Jan have continued to do through various ministry opportunities. Having seen firsthand the wondrous eternity people give up in exchange for a few years of earthly pleasure, he's determined to spend his life helping them make a different choice.

"God loves us so much and has put so much effort into what he's prepared for us. I see now that I'm living my life for future generations and for heaven as well. I want heaven to be proud of my life. That is a profound responsibility."

30

THE SCARS TO PROVE IT

After being electrocuted and pronounced dead, Art Walters
returned to life—and the miracles didn't stop there.

On the morning of September 18, 1971, Art Walters rolled out of bed as he usually did—straight onto his knees. Having escaped a few years ago, with God's help, from a dead-end life of addiction to drugs and alcohol, he knew better than anyone how easy it would be to let temptation drag him back into the past. It had become his habit to avoid that possibility by dedicating each day to the Lord right from the beginning.

He'd been married for two years to Vicki, a woman who shared his dream of reaching out to street people, especially those whose lives had also been ravaged by drugs and alcohol. Together they had helped create *Casa de Vida* (House of Life), a Christian halfway house in Santa Barbara, California, whose mission was to assist people trying to break free from the downward spiral of homelessness and addiction. As live-in counselors, Art and Vicki provided shelter, job training, and spiritual guidance to anyone who sought it.

To help make ends meet, residents often took odd jobs around the community—landscaping, painting, or minor renovations and repairs. On that day Art was planning to supervise several ongoing projects. But first, on his knees in the bedroom, his former lifestyle came to mind. He thought of all his old friends who were still partying, ruining relationships, living only for themselves.

"I asked God to burn bridges in my life that morning," he said. "I asked him to get rid of everything in my life that might still tempt me to turn back. I guess it really is true you have to be careful what you pray for."

Later he set out on his rounds under a gorgeous, sunny blue sky. His first task: Check in with Bud, a Casa de Vida resident who'd become a believer two weeks earlier. Bud was tackling a variety of odd jobs at a local motel being remodeled, and the manager had offered an almost-new fifteen-foot TV antenna to the halfway house—provided they would remove it from her roof. After a quick assessment, Art and Bud decided to take her up on the deal.

With a stepladder the men climbed onto a wooden trellis covering the patio alongside the building. From there they stepped onto the clay tile roof and made their way upward to the antenna, attached to a long pole that fitted into an even longer one anchored in the ground below. All they had to do was lift the top portion free and lower it down. They took positions on opposite sides, got a firm grip, and lifted. According to plan, it came free.

But the antenna on top was heavier than they imagined. Furthermore, its weight wasn't balanced—and the pole slowly began tilting to one side. They strained with all their might to hold it upright but lacked the leverage to counteract its growing momentum.

"I don't have it!" Bud shouted.

Art didn't either.

As if in slow motion the antenna toppled onto a cluster of high-voltage electrical wires strung too close to the building. The force of the impact broke through the wires and sent the live ends falling to the rooftop. Two cylindrical transformers atop the utility pole exploded, showering the roof with sparks. A ball of fire traveled down the pole and engulfed Art and Bud in flames. The repulsive electrical force threw them both like rag dolls onto the tiles.

Art was instantly knocked unconscious. And his clothes were on fire.

———⊗⊗⊗———

"The last thing I remember," Art recalled, "was holding on to the pole and watching my hands start to bend over with it. Then everything went black, like I had been shoved into a dark closet."

He believes he died at that moment. "I was still awake and aware, I just couldn't see anything," he said.

Suddenly he felt a cool breeze on his face, as if a fan had turned on. He looked to his left and saw something in the distance coming toward him—or maybe *he* was moving toward *it*. He had the impression of looking through binoculars and trying to focus on the image as it drew closer. Then he saw clearly that the object was his own body. Looking down at himself, lying on the roof, charred and burning, he *knew* he was dead.

"Then I looked to my right and saw the huge chest of a man, from the neck down to the hands. I knew right then I was in the presence of the Lord. It was like he was too big for the picture frame. His chest took up the whole sky. I watched as his hands scooped up my body, held it for a few seconds, and then set me back down. I could feel his wonderful presence in those hands and in that embrace."

When Jesus put him back down, Art awoke in his body again—and stood up. He was surprised to see he was now off the roof and surrounded by fire department and ambulance crews. He looked down at his horribly burned body.

Then he passed out.

—————

Like Art, Bud had been thrown down by the high-voltage force. His first thought upon seeing Art's unconscious body was that his friend was dead. The sparking wires dancing wildly across the rooftop occasionally made contact with Bud's torso and legs. It occurred to him that he also would be dead soon.

Though his relationship with God was so new, he cried out, "Jesus!" He thought it would be his last word. Instead, a surge of strength passed through his body and stood him on his feet. He patted out the flames on Art's shirt and pants. He had severe burns over 30 percent of his body, but he dragged his friend to the roof's edge, to the patio covering where they'd climbed up. Leaving him there, Bud descended the ladder. At the bottom he tried to figure out the best way to get Art off the roof.

When he looked back up, Bud was astonished to see a man standing on the roof. He held Art's limp body in his arms and was handing him down the ladder. Bud took his friend and laid him on the ground. When he looked up again the man had vanished. He later told Art he was certain it was an angel of God, sent to help.

Emergency medical technicians arrived and pronounced Art dead. They estimated he'd been dead at least ten minutes. He had second- and third-degree burns over 70 percent of his body—and no measurable signs of life.

Bud sat and began to repeatedly pray, "Please, Jesus, don't let him die!"

At that moment Art abruptly stood up from the stretcher as if someone had lifted him to his feet. He looked around, then at himself—and collapsed. The EMTs sprang to action. They packed his body in ice gathered from the motel ice machine. On the way to the hospital his heart stopped beating five times. Each time he was revived.

Over the next three weeks Art Walters had every reason to wish he'd remained dead. Once he regained consciousness he was in constant, excruciating pain. The renowned British plastic surgeon John Chapple "coincidentally" was on duty when he was rushed in, so he got excellent care. But there was nothing anyone could do to diminish the agony of his deep, widespread burns.

The prognosis was not good. Doctors told Art and Vicki that he could die of fluid loss, infection, even exhaustion from treatment. If he survived, he might be paralyzed or might have heart or brain damage. Certainly there'd be severe scarring over his entire body, including his face. In fact, Dr. Chapple had already decided that the facial damage warranted immediate surgery.

"I heard that and visualized myself as a hideous monster for the rest of my life," Art said. "I cried out to God, 'What are you doing to me?'"

God answered with a promise—and a question. *"I can heal you completely. But would you be willing to carry these scars for my glory, as a testimony to what I can do?"*

Art agreed, though he didn't know exactly what that meant for his future.

God said, *"As a sign to you, I will heal your face so there is no scarring."*

———

The next morning Dr. Chapple took one look at Art's face and canceled the surgery.

"He came in, looked at me, and in that British accent said, 'My, how remarkably your face has healed overnight.'"

Still the pain went on. The rest of his body remained in critical condition.

Every day he underwent the horror of having his bandages changed. Nurses stood him upright using his specially designed mechanical bed frame. Then he spent half an hour stepping away from the mattress that had stuck to his seared flesh. Once free, he was taken by wheelchair to a whirlpool and immersed in body-temperature water. There he endured more agony as nurses pulled away the old bandages to prepare his body for new ones.

"I screamed and screamed night and day," he said. "I couldn't eat or drink. I couldn't sleep. It was horrible. Not knowing when the pain would end was the worst part."

Doctors expected Art to be in the hospital undergoing treatments for at least three months. After four weeks things were not going well. Infection was a constant concern, as was keeping his body hydrated. He was allowed no visitors except Vicki, dressed in full protective clothing so that only her eyes were visible to him. On top of everything else he battled growing despair.

A bright spot in his day came when a nurse would snatch a few fleeting moments to read to him from Scripture. One verse in particular gripped his heart: "No temptation has seized you except what is common to man. And God is faithful; he will not let you be tempted beyond what you can bear. But when you are tempted, he will also provide a way out so that you can stand up under it" (1 Corinthians 10:13).

A way out. That sounded good. "I knew God was telling me to keep looking for the way out he'd provided and not to give up," he said.

Several weeks into recovery, Art spotted greenish smoke pouring into his room around the door. His first panicked thought was that the building was on fire. But he quickly realized that an evil spirit had entered and was filling the room with thick, oppressive smoke.

"It was a satanic presence. I started hearing a voice in my head that said, 'Wouldn't you like to be done with this pain? It could be over in a matter of seconds. Go on, you can do it.'"

Art's right arm had been burned from his armpit to his fingertips, but he somehow managed to reach for a pair of scissors on the bedside table. He picked them up and felt an unseen force pushing his hand toward his body.

He began to pray. "I'm a Christian! I serve God. I know this isn't right."

Still something pressed on his hand, moving it closer to his chest. He kept praying—then felt another force take hold of his clenched fist and push in the opposite direction. He felt it was the Holy Spirit responding to his prayers.

"I was in the middle of a spiritual battle, a tug-of-war, with my life on the line. Then all of a sudden the room was filled with light. I looked and saw the Lord Jesus standing at the foot of my bed. He was radiant and beautiful! He smiled at me and put his hand on the end of my bed. Instantly I fell asleep—a miracle in itself, as I'd been unable to sleep for at least four weeks until then."

The next day when nurses entered the room to begin the daily bandage-changing ordeal, they were astonished to find Art asleep. As usual they proceeded to stand his bed up and to free his skin from the mattress.

"This time, as I stepped away from the bed, I closed my eyes and saw the face of Jesus smiling at me, just like he had the night before. He told me, 'I am the way out.' I knew he was talking about the verse in First Corinthians. I kept my eyes closed, looking at his face. It seemed like only a few seconds."

But when he opened them again, his body was already wrapped in fresh bandages—without a trip to the whirlpool. The nurses had painlessly removed all the old covering and replaced it with new.

"From that moment on things began to turn around. Surgeries were more effective, infection reversed course, and the pain was more manageable. Contrary to the doctor's prediction, I was able to walk out of the hospital two weeks later. I looked like Frankenstein, but I was walking."

Art's road to full recovery was still arduous and lasted many months. Yet he did recover. As for Bud, he overcame his injuries as well. Though Art and Vicki lost contact with him over the years, they'll never forget how his remarkable faith and fervent prayer brought Art through the fire that day.

Not even Vicki can see a trace of scarring on Art's face now. And true to his other promise, God has used Art's remarkable story many times through the years to draw people to him. The couple has continued in full-time service as missionaries to Central America and in various U.S. churches and ministries.

He sums up: "I was given a gift—more time on earth to help people and to serve God. Each day is an opportunity I try to use to the fullest."

MORE MIRACULOUS MOMENTS

Further Glimpses of God's Grace and Greatness

One of the great delights of researching and writing a book on miracles is hearing from so many who know without doubt that God intervened in their lives. When we put out a call for these experiences, we received stacks more than we could include here. Poring over each story, we were astonished at the frequency and the variety with which God demonstrates his power.

As it was difficult to decide on the stories to feature among so many, we'd like at least to present several more in brief—even more confirmation that God participates in his children's lives regularly and remarkably.

Miracle on Jefferson Street

When I was pastor of a Phoenix church, our members collected thirty-five blankets to give to homeless individuals.

What began as a simple service project turned into a bona fide miracle.

On December 22, 1994, the air was crisp and getting colder, so as I traveled on I-17 in the church van, I asked God to make those thirty-five blankets warmer than ever and to be received by those who needed them most. Arriving where I knew homeless people congregated, I saw about ten people a block away, huddled around an open fire in a barrel. I turned the van and cautiously approached.

"Would you like a blanket to keep warm tonight?" I asked.

"Yeah!" was the response from one man as he made his way toward me. I handed him a blanket, and he expressed his gratitude. Then there was another hand by the window, and I turned for another blanket. Next three hands clamored, and I turned to get the blankets. Soon the crowd of ten had swelled to a mob. There were too many hands to count, and the van was surrounded. Admittedly, I was glad I had all the doors locked.

Suddenly I thought, *I don't have enough for everyone.* Panic began to set in. But I could feel something all around me, a clear sense of God's presence. Peace displaced the panic.

"I'm new to the streets. Can I please have a blanket?" This was a voice so tender and sweet it caused me to turn toward it. The request was from a woman who looked out of place amid the backdrop of the reaching hands.

Before I could respond, a man's deep voice said, "Please give her one. She really needs it." Her hands were not reaching as the others were, for they were tight across her chest to keep warm.

I remember thinking that the light jacket she had was not going to keep her warm through the colder nights. I wished I had a coat to give her. I handed her the last new blanket, still in its packaging from the manufacturer.

"May I have a new blanket too?" asked a tall man with a beard badly in need of a trim. Desperation filled his eyes, and I said, "Brother, I really wish I had some more new ones to give you, but that was the last new blanket."

As I said the word *blanket,* the words of Jesus came to mind: "Truly I tell you, whatever you did for one of the least of these brothers and sisters of mine, you did for me" (Matthew 25:40). I remember thinking, *This man is Jesus. That woman is Jesus.*

As I turned for an old blanket, obviously used and worn, I saw to my surprise two *new* blankets on the floor. As I picked them up, it dawned on me that those new ones hadn't been there before. I'd given them all out—I was sure of it. Again I turned for more old blankets, and now there were two *more* new ones in the same spot. This happened several times: I'd reach for old blankets only to find additional new ones.

Moisture began to form in my eyes. A blink released the tears down my cheeks. I tried to hide my emotion from the unknowing crowd, but knew I was unsuccessful when a man in tattered clothes asked, "Sir, are you all right?"

I quickly said, "Couldn't be better" as a smile crossed my face.

With the last hand awaiting a blanket, I gave out the last one. I started with thirty-five blankets and I gave out at least fifty. And I know how.

As I put the van in gear I heard several people say, "God bless you, mister." Humbled in the presence of God, I replied, "He already did."

Driving back to the church, I said to myself, *It wasn't* Miracle on 34th Street, *but it was a miracle on Jefferson Avenue.* I thought of Jesus feeding the five thousand, and I thought of Jesus "blanketing" the fifty. What a profound joy to participate in a miracle.

—James Taylor, Norman, Oklahoma

Battered but Not Bruised

Visiting Atlanta for a convention in October 2002, I arranged to meet several acquaintances at a downtown restaurant one evening. The weather was crisp and pleasant, so I decided to walk the half mile—which soon turned into a mile, and then another, as I became confused and then hopelessly lost.

I found myself in a run-down area. I looked for a taxi but didn't see one. I called the restaurant for directions and realized it was a long trek back—I was already late, the sky was nearly dark, and the streets were practically deserted. Frustration at my lousy planning rapidly turned to fear. I quickened my pace.

As I passed a shadowy alley, three men—tough-looking, smelling of booze and more—leapt out and grabbed me, shoved me against a wall, and demanded my wallet. Not about to argue, I reached into my coat pocket, but they must have thought I had a weapon. One, brandishing a bat, proceeded to wind up and belt the back of my head three times.

I crumpled like a rag doll as they crowded over me. I expected searing pain or a fade to black. But I felt only alert and pain-free. Then I thought I must be going on adrenaline and soon would be unconscious. Wrong again.

I played possum as the muggers rummaged and took my wallet, phone, and watch. I was glad to let them have the stuff so long as they left. A moment later they turned and sprinted away.

Waiting to make sure they wouldn't return, I sat up warily, gingerly. Shouldn't I be harmed, if not dead? Shouldn't I have a concussion, or at least a headache? I felt perfectly normal. I touched the back of my head, all over, and didn't even find a bruise.

I flew home to Tallahassee the next morning and immediately went to my doctor, explaining the attack in detail. He checked me out carefully and found nothing wrong. Precautionary X-rays came back clean.

The thugs who robbed me got a few hundred dollars' worth of valuables, but I got something priceless: the assurance that God does intervene in this sick, broken world. Specifically, he intervenes in the lives of sick, broken people and those affected by sick, broken people.

I have no doubt I received a miracle. Why me? Why was I protected when most people who are assaulted suffer terrible consequences? I've asked that many times, and I have no answer. I can't explain it. I can only say with humbleness, "Thank you, God. Thank you for protecting me."

—Joseph Cendejas, Tallahassee, Florida

Voice of Caution

As pastor of a church in southwestern Michigan, I encountered a miraculous experience one foggy Easter morning on my way to sunrise service. As I approached a curve in the road, I heard a man's voice say unmistakably, "Slow down." It was so real and clear that I actually responded by answering "Okay" and lifting my foot off the accelerator.

Chuckling at the unusual experience, I began once more to speed up. The voice spoke again, this time with more intensity: "No. Keep slowing down."

I took my foot completely off the gas as the car continued to decelerate. As I rounded the corner, my headlights illuminated through the fog a tottering elderly man crossing the road, headed for his mailbox. Had I continued at the same speed as before "the voice" spoke, the old gentleman would have been square in the middle of my lane when I got there.

231

He'd just reached the shoulder when I passed. At that same moment an oncoming van passed, cutting off any escape route had I needed to swerve left to save the man. Had I swerved right I'd have crashed into a large oak tree.

With shaking knees, I thanked God for a miraculous preservation of at least one precious life and perhaps more. It may seem a relatively "small" incident of divine intervention, but it had big implications for those involved.

—Clark Cothern, Ypsilanti, Michigan

From Sorrow to Solace

My husband, Snow, died at a football game, enjoying the action on the field one minute, gone to be with the Lord the next. We'd been sitting on the fifty-yard line, watching with interest, when suddenly, softly, he called my name and then leaned over to lie across the stadium seats.

In just moments his eyes rolled back, and I could see nothing but white on the back of his eyeballs. Out of the crowd came our own family doctor, who'd been nearby, as well as EMS-trained people, nurses, and other medical personnel. They tried to revive Snow via mouth-to-mouth resuscitation, heart massage, and defibrillation. Unsuccessful, they raced him away in the ambulance kept on-site for possible football-related injuries.

At age forty-nine he'd had a massive heart attack. He was pronounced dead on arrival at the hospital. We went home that night without him.

Some family members slept in my room. I climbed under the covers with my daughter, Patsy, who was asleep in her white canopy bed. A soft light shined from the hallway.

When I closed my eyes I began my usual prayer of thanks for the day. As I silently began, "Dear Lord," I felt a hand before my eyes and heard—or sensed—a voice that said, "No."

Startled, I opened my eyes. "Patsy," I said aloud, "are you playing a joke on me?" She was breathing deeply and obviously asleep.

I closed my eyes again, thinking, *Of course I shouldn't pray as usual tonight. It's the darkest day of my life. I need more honest, sincere words than my bedtime prayer.*

I started again, this time mustering all the courage I had to invoke the Spirit of God: "Almighty God!" Again I felt the hand across my face and a "No" that resounded through my spirit.

I opened my eyes once more. No one. Nothing there.

Upset, I prayed, "Lord, you can't desert me tonight. I need you more than ever. You must help me tonight. I need you." Then I tentatively began, "Dear God, please assure me that Snow is right there with you."

My spirit opened, and I felt the presence of both God and Snow. I knew for sure my husband was in heaven—no doubt remained. What a reassurance for a wife and mother of two teenagers that she could make it through the rest of her life without her solid-rock husband. He was with his heavenly Father, and I knew absolutely that he was alive and well.

After Snow's funeral, his best friend, Allen, and his family came home with us. Amid the hubbub of welcoming guests and preparing snacks in the kitchen, he drew me aside. "Something unusual happened to me today," he said. "At the graveside I looked down at a baby's headstone nearby with a little lamb on top of it. It reminded me of Craig."

Allen and Dianne had lost their three-year-old son in a freak accident the first day Allen had been with the child after his wife had returned to work. Both of these grief-stricken

233

but believing parents had handled the child's death well, as far as I knew, yet Allen told another story. He said that after Craig died he was plagued by the fear that when he got to heaven his son would greet him with the words: "Where were you, Daddy, when I needed you? You were there a few minutes before, but when I was in distress, why didn't you see me? Why didn't you rescue me?"

"To tell the truth," he said, "I decided I couldn't face Craig. I couldn't handle the hurt and disappointment in his eyes because his daddy let him down. After that I turned my back on God, doing anything I could to make him refuse my entrance into heaven."

"I'm so sorry, Allen," I said.

"But today something happened. As I looked at the lamb headstone and thought of my precious Craig, I felt a tap on my shoulder. Thinking it was a pallbearer who knew how close I was to Snow, I turned to say 'I'm okay. I'll be all right.' To my surprise, no one was there. In fact, no one was within ten or twelve feet of me!"

He smiled and looked me in the eye. "Edna, I heard Snow! I'm not going to tell anyone else because they'll think I'm crazy, but I know I heard him. I know his voice. It was him! Snow said to me, 'You can come on home, Allen, anytime you want to. Don't be afraid of heaven or facing Craig. I've already straightened that out. Everything is all right now.' Then he was gone."

A moment later he added, "I had to tell you what Snow said. He's alive. He's in heaven."

"I know," I said. "I already know."

Assurance about heaven may come in unusual ways. God can use such incidents to bring us comfort and confidence about the world beyond this one.

—Edna Ellison, Spartanburg, South Carolina

Prepare for Impact

For my seventeenth birthday in 1971, my parents bought me my first car—a powder blue 1963 Oldsmobile F-85. I sure was proud. I washed and waxed it every Saturday morning.

One summer afternoon I drove away from my home in the Cincinnati suburb of Norwood. I'd just gotten a green light and was turning left off Worth Avenue onto Rhode Island Street, when I noticed a car coming from my left. I assumed he would stop for the red. He didn't.

Maybe he was changing radio stations. I really don't know. Regardless, he was speeding through the light on a no-miss, T-bone collision course. It was not only a possibility but a certainty that the front of his car would slam into my driver's-side door.

My experiences over the years have taught me that people tend to use the word *miracle* too loosely. But I was there, and *miracle* is the only word fit to use. Only the hand of God could have prevented that sure catastrophe.

The other car *literally* passed through mine like Casper the friendly ghost passes through walls. As it did, the other driver, ostensibly a boy about my age, turned, and our eyes met. His face was no more than eighteen *inches* from mine, and I'll never forget his look of complete shock. I must have appeared the same way to him.

In this instant, time seemed to slow considerably. Immediately afterward both of us stopped, got out, and stood, just staring at each other. If I knew who he was and where to find him—I don't know whatever became of him—he would tell you the same.

After a few moments I got back into my car and drove two blocks to a Sohio gas station. I pulled in and parked, sitting in stunned silence, trying to grasp what had happened. I'd been raised in church, and I realized I'd just experienced divine intervention.

As I got out and examined my car, I knew what had occurred, yet many years went by before I ever told anyone. I was truly amazed by the magnitude of the event, but I figured people would think I was being sensationalistic.

In time I became a Southern Baptist clergyman, and I've shared this from the pulpit with two different congregations. Some have nodded in polite disbelief; there were others who hoped it was true but simply could not accept it. Humanly speaking they're correct, yet, as Jesus said, "with God all things are possible" (Mark 10:27). Several people from both churches came up to me afterward, said they believed it, and then proceeded to share miracle stories of their own. I believed every one of them because I know what happened to me one day in Cincinnati long ago.

—Victor Cooper, Bokeelia, Florida

The Boy Beneath a Bus

On May 6, 2011, our family experienced the single worst day of our lives. Unexpectedly, it also ended as our most miraculous day.

That Friday morning began like any other school day: hurrying to get the kids ready and out the door to the bus. On school mornings, Rachel is not only Mom but also bus driver of a local route for Union Grove Christian School. Our three oldest children, Stanley, Angela, and Torrey, ride the bus with Mom each day.

At 7:40, when the bus stopped at the drop-off spot, the children filed off as usual. The older children headed directly into the school building while the younger ones crossed in front of the bus to a coned area to wait for the bell. Torrey,

236

age six, also stepped off and walked. But instead of going straight over to the coned area, he unexpectedly crouched, apparently pretending to be a favorite movie character (as he's known to do). In that position, Torrey was hidden from sight and did not notice that the bus had begun to move forward.

At this moment, Angela saw what was happening and realized Mom could not see Torrey. She yelled for him to lie down so the bus would pass over him. This moment was the first miracle—Angela's urgent instruction alerted Torrey to what was happening. He managed to get down as the bus moved over him. A moment later, when he saw the opening between the front and back wheels, he tried to scramble to safety. Unable to move fast enough, the double rear wheels ran over the entire midsection of his thin little body. School buses typically weigh around 25,000 pounds, and this was on top of a boy weighing sixty.

Feeling the unexpected bump, Rachel stopped immediately. Running to the front of the bus, she saw Torrey lying beneath the rear wheels. She rushed inside the building to get someone to call 9–1–1. Immediately, people hurried to help and pushed the bus off Torrey.

Parents, staff, and children began to pray. The drop-off became a sort of "ground zero" for our family, friends, and school community.

Soon, Torrey regained consciousness. He suffered major lacerations and bruising, two broken collarbones, a chipped hip bone, four broken ribs, and broken blood vessels in his eyes and face. Still, he was conscious for the entire ambulance ride and life flight to Children's Hospital in Milwaukee.

The hours that followed were filled with tears, prayers, meetings with surgeons, hugs from family and friends, emergency surgery, and more prayers. Even as we traveled to one hospital and then followed the helicopter to the next, we were overwhelmed with the prayers and love of God's family. We began to receive calls and messages from people around the globe who dropped what they were doing to gather together in prayer for our little boy. We believe it is those prayers that made all the difference. Torrey's injuries had been lessened by his backpack, which absorbed much of the tires' pressure. Amazingly, no major organs were damaged.

After eight days in the hospital, Torrey was released with not so much as a cast or a bandage. His bones healed so quickly that the breaks were hard to detect at his next doctor appointment. A week and a half after the accident, he was able to visit his class at school. After missing only two weeks, he rejoined his class for the rest of the school year.

The emotional toll on a child his age is also a big concern. Eventually, Torrey was able to say, "It's not that I wanted to be run over, but I know God wanted lots of people to hear about Jesus and how to be saved." He has no lasting effect from the accident except a heightened knowledge of how big our God is. Truly we serve an awesome God!

—Josh and Rachel Steele, Union Grove, Wisconsin

An Open-and-Closed Case

I serve as a chaplain at the City of Hope National Medical Center. In April 2010, I received an urgent page: A woman in the surgical waiting area asked that I come and pray with her as soon as possible.

Arriving a few minutes later, I recognized the woman, who was there with her college-age daughter. We had talked before, during one of her cancer-stricken husband's previous admissions.

They were devout Christians, but she was very nervous about this potentially dangerous procedure. She explained that he was already in surgery. Would I please pray with them right now?

I said I'd be more than happy to, and amid several others in the waiting room, we formed a "circle of love" and joined hands and hearts as I briefly led them in asking God to guide the surgeon, protect her husband, and comfort them as they waited. I gave them my card and asked them to keep me posted.

The next morning I got a call from the wife. All she could say was, "It's a miracle! It's a miracle!" She was so excited I could hardly get any more information. I asked if her husband had been moved to the ICU, as is protocol, and she said yes.

Walking into the man's room later that day, I saw him sitting up and looking remarkably good for just having had major cancer surgery. He immediately said, with a huge smile, "It's a miracle! It's a miracle!"

Still not sure what had happened, I asked him to explain. He told me the surgeon had gone into the OR, where he was already sedated and prepped, with CT scans clearly showing the tumors to be removed. However, when the surgeon opened him up, not one tumor was present. There was no sign of them even though the evidence was right there on the scans!

Not knowing what else to do, the surgeon closed the incision and sent him to recovery. Later, meeting with the patient and his family, he said, "Well, the chemotherapy agent was continuing to work, and it must have completely reduced the tumors to nothing." That was the only human explanation the doctor could find for this miracle of God's grace.

The family and I shared a celebration and wonderful time of prayer and praising God. I left marveling at his healing grace.

—Terry Irish, Glendora, California

Lifeguard on Duty

When I was eight my mom took us kids to the beach for a day. I couldn't swim so she told me to wade but stay where she could see me. It didn't take long for me to wander all the way out into the fishing area. Somehow the large pier drew me to it, far out of Mom's view.

A man was there, wearing rubber waders, holding a big fishing pole. His big tackle box sat nearby on the shore. I said I must have walked too far by accident, and he told me to go back because my mom was worried about me.

He was right. Mom *was* very upset and set closer boundaries.

So I went back in to splash around the same wading area. Nothing new—until the sand beneath my feet disappeared. I'd fallen into a huge hole, unseen under the surface.

I thrashed and gulped seawater. As I struggled, I discovered that moving my arms down in unison propelled me to the top for air.

I yelled for help, and Mom rushed to me. But every time she got near she also fell into the hole. She cried out, "God, help me!"

Right then the fisherman I'd met earlier reached out and grabbed me. He handed me over to my mom. After she embraced me she turned to thank him . . . but he was gone. In a moment. We never found him to thank him.

I'm convinced he was an angel. How else could he arrive and vanish so instantly? Why did he appear right after Mom's

240

prayer? Why couldn't we find him after he rescued me? I'll find out the answers someday in heaven.

—John Wastlund, Osawatomie, Kansas

You Snooze, You . . . Win

In July 2006, I cruised home in my old '84 Corvette to La Mesa, California, from a lot I own near Julian. It was warm. The radio played. The engine's hum and the wind's white noise were rhythmic and hypnotic. There was nobody anywhere near me on Highway 8 eastbound. I'm embarrassed to admit I nodded off.

Coming down the grade from Alpine into El Cajon, I woke to a crash and a jolt, behind the wheel, still doing over 70 mph. I had changed lanes and smacked into an ambulance right beside me.

I don't know how many seconds I was out, but I do know that not one other vehicle was in sight on that stretch. What's more, to the right of my car was a sheer rock face; to the left was a sharp drop-off onto oncoming lanes. The ambulance "appeared" and served as a guardrail to keep me from wrecking.

No doubt God had intervened to save my life. I was convinced, but I also realized it would sound farfetched when I described it. I'm embarrassed (again!) to admit I lied to my wife, Traci, about the accident. I told her my car and the ambulance had merged into the same lane at the same time. The minimal damage to my car was covered by insurance. It's still on my driving record.

That was the end of it—until Traci started having a dream. Though she'd never before dreamed that God himself was talking to her, she now dreamed (the same thing three times before she told me) that God was saying he was helping her in dramatic fashion and yet she wasn't grateful for it.

241

As she told me the dream, I immediately felt convicted. I confessed that I believed God had saved my life a few weeks earlier by placing an ambulance (of all vehicles) between me and a high-speed death. It all made sense.

By this I also learned that I am not the star in this play; Traci is. I'm a player put here to help my wife and family, not the other way around. God came to her, not to me, to convey what he had done and to get my attention. I am thrilled and humbled to receive his attention in any respect.

—Carl Hoppes, La Mesa, California

Financial Aid From the "Bank of Heaven"

At a church I pastored, a young couple attended with their four children, participating faithfully, tithing regularly. The man had a job in a local factory.

One evening they came to see me. They had purchased a house in the past year to meet their expanding family needs. They thought they'd checked out all the costs involved before committing. However, to their shock, an unforeseen assessment had just been levied on their property for $2,000, due within the month. They didn't know what to do.

I didn't know either. I had less than $100 in my discretionary account. I said a prayer with them, asking God to provide.

A couple of days later, I received a call from a wealthy member who said he wanted to catch up on his tithe. He explained that he hadn't fully tithed the past few years while paying his children's way through college. He intended to make a donation of $10,000!

Right before the Sunday service, he walked in and said, "As I was writing out the check, it occurred to me that you might like part of this to go into your discretionary fund. Would that be all right?"

I assured him it would be appreciated. He handed me a check for $2,000.

I could hardly wait for the service to end. When it did, I grabbed the couple and led them into a side room. "You're not going to believe this," I said. "I have the money for you." I explained that someone had given me the exact amount they needed.

Needless to say they were overjoyed. And while I never told the donor who they were, he likewise was overjoyed to know that God had used him to bless a Christian family in need.

—Richard Blank, Onsted, Michigan

Gone Without a Trace

Our son Luke was a four-year-old boy who loved sports, with two older brothers to play with. In June of 2011, Luke had a suspicious "bump" come up on his right temple. We thought that the bump had resulted from smacking his head on something. Like many active boys, Luke often banged into things around the house as he played ball or goofed off.

We monitored the bump for a few days, and the swelling didn't go down. We took Luke to his pediatrician, who thought it might be a cyst. Over the next few weeks, the bump began to grow rapidly, around one centimeter per week. In July, the pediatrician sent us to a surgeon at Nemours Children's Clinic in Jacksonville, Florida.

The surgeon also thought Luke had a cyst. She wanted to watch it for the next three weeks to see if the cyst would go away naturally. Because it was between the skull and cranium, we all hoped the body would absorb it instead of having to go through surgery to remove it. But at the end of the three weeks, the bump had hardened. Tests were ordered, including a CT scan. The results were distressing: The scan suggested

243

that Luke had Langerhans Cell Histiocytosis (LCH), a rare disease affecting only five out of every one million children. We were immediately referred to an oncologist, who ordered another CT scan, an MRI, X-rays, skeletal survey, and blood work.

All of the tests confirmed the diagnosis of LCH. The oncologist and a neurosurgeon explained that Luke had a tumor on his skull that was attacking his body. It had eaten an inch-long hole through his skull to his brain. There was no sign that the brain had been affected, but we wouldn't know for sure until surgery. The surgeon was going to remove the tumor and repair his skull with a type of calcium deposit or a metal plate. A plate was preferred because of the width of the hole in the skull. When we asked if it were possible for the bone to grow back on its own, the surgeon said no. Surgery was set for November 2, 2011, and thereafter Luke would face a minimum of six months of chemotherapy.

After hearing the devastating news, we returned home. Luke was brave, and he prayed each day for God to "heal my bump." Over the next few weeks, Luke became sick, developing a fever. He was on multiple antibiotics to try to get his body stable enough to perform the surgery. Luke also complained of minor aches and pains in his legs and stomach.

A week and a half before surgery, a second bump appeared about two inches from the first bump. We immediately called the doctor, who said there was no need to put Luke through the testing again at this point. He said he would look at it when Luke came in for surgery. He would resect it and repair the skull in that place as well, if necessary.

The morning of November 2, 2011, we drove to Wolfson Children's Hospital in Jacksonville. Luke was called back to prep for surgery at 12:30. The neurosurgeon came in and talked with us about what would happen during surgery. He located the second bump and marked the intended places of incision on Luke's head with a marker. The anesthesiologist came in and went over procedures and risks. Then the doctor excused himself for a few minutes. When he returned, he said the operating room was not yet available, so he would send Luke for another CT scan in order to get a better look at the second tumor. He said it would only take about ten minutes.

Luke went for his scan and returned to the prepping area. The anesthesiologist and OR nurse were waiting for us. The doctor reviewed the new CT scan and then excused himself to radiology again. When he returned, he placed scans taken in September and November side by side on the screen to compare the two. He showed us where the tumor was and where the skull had been destructed.

On the new scan, there was no tumor, and the skull had repaired itself. Luke's bone had grown back.

"I can't explain it," the doctor said.

We immediately told him we could explain it: the power of prayer and the mercy of God!

I know in my heart that God heard our cries of desperation. Many people were on their knees praying, and we are humbled and elated that God chose to heal him. The Lord must have great and mighty things in store for Luke. May we never forget the absolute awesome feeling of the power and presence of God.

—Brad Hooks, Waycross, Georgia

"Turn Off the Radio and Pray"

One beautiful sunny day in July 1992, at 5:30 PM, I was driving my Oldsmobile Cutlass Supreme south on I-35, headed from Oklahoma City to Norman. I was scheduled to teach a class at Southern Nazarene University.

I was listening to sports talk radio and not exactly focused on spiritual things at the time, when a voice suddenly spoke to me: "Turn off the radio and pray for your safety." The urgent words were so perfectly clear that it sounded as if someone were in the car with me.

Despite the unmistakable warning, I was more puzzled than anything and continued as before. Then the voice said again, "Turn off the radio and pray for your safety." Feeling almost foolish, I did exactly that: "Lord, if I am in danger, please surround me with your protection. I leave this in your hands."

Two minutes later a teenager in a Trans Am came scream-ing out of a parking lot and into the street (I'd just merged onto an exit ramp at Norman). He nearly hit me broadside. I did a complete 360 in the road at 65 mph. Two other cars ended up in a ditch and on the road's shoulder, respectively.

As I continued to drive, the voice came again and said, "Never forget that I am not only your Creator and Savior but I am also your Protector."

If I hadn't been watching for something to occur, which I was because of that voice, I'd have been hit broadside and probably killed. When I got home around 11:00 PM, I told my wife, Vickie, about the incident, and we agreed to wake our two kids to tell them how God had protected me.

—Steve Stearman, Oklahoma City, Oklahoma

No Oil Shortage

I'd been invited to speak to a combined group of Catholics and Protestants in a local Catholic church by a friend who's a nun. I spoke to a group of fifty about the blind beggar Jesus healed, and I encouraged them to see themselves as the beggar coming to the Lord with their requests and needs. I closed by offering the opportunity to receive prayer, and all fifty people responded.

Since I like to anoint with oil when I pray for others, I pulled my small vial from my pocket and quickly realized it was almost empty. I knew it would not be enough, so I asked if anyone had more. A person in the back thought he had some in his car and left the service to get it.

Meanwhile I started praying and anointing the people, one by one. I'd prayed for half and, sure enough, by the twenty-fifth person my oil was gone. I tried pounding the bottle on my hand to get a last drop, but it was bone-dry.

An aisle separated me from the other twenty-five, and as I walked over to pray for the next group I thought, *I can just keep praying and go through the motions of anointing each one. They'll never know if I have oil or not.* Then I asked myself if this would be deceitful. I paused, not knowing what to do.

At that same instant the man returned and asked if I still needed oil. I said yes and held up the bottle to show it was empty. To my surprise, and to the surprise of the few people sitting close to me, the bottle was now half full. The one closest to me called out, "I just saw your bottle fill up with oil!"

I did not see it happen, but, nevertheless, there it was. So I just kept praying and anointing as if this were all normal. The tiny vial didn't run out for months, and we used it many, many times. Everybody wanted to be anointed with the "oil from heaven."

I asked the Lord what this incident meant and have thought on it a lot. Perhaps it just meant that I had a need and he met it. I also realized that he is closer than I sometimes think, and he cares about the small details of our lives.

—Don Shafer, Anchorage, Alaska

A Dream Come True

My Grandma Morgan was like a guardian angel to me, my biggest prayer warrior and supporter. When I was diagnosed with learning disabilities as a child, she always encouraged me and believed in me. Though experts told my parents I probably wouldn't be able to finish junior high, Grandma always pushed me to achieve. Her vibrant red hair was like a flaming torch blazing trails for me as she constantly challenged and motivated me.

With encouragement from my parents and grandma, I not only finished high school but also graduated from college with a bachelor's degree in behavioral science, going on to work for many years with delinquent juveniles. Then I felt God wanted me to change fields and be trained in emergency medical services. Once again Grandma cheered me on, encouraging me to follow my dream. Today I'm a registered paramedic, performing ambulance and helicopter critical care.

I was devastated when I got the news that Grandma had cancer. She suffered for several years, and then word came that she was nearing the end. Since she lived in Wichita, Kansas, and I in Bartlesville, Oklahoma, I made sure to visit many times during her illness.

Early Sunday morning, October 29, 2006, I woke from a deep sleep. I lay there awestruck, reflecting on a vivid dream. I remembered finding myself in a bright, wonderful, indescribable light. It was warm, and I heard beautiful voices. A multitude of people whose faces seemed too bright to behold was standing around one person in the middle of the group. The crowd was parted down one side by an even greater, indescribably bright light. I knew that light was coming from the throne and that Jesus was at its center.

As I looked closer, I began to recognize some in the circle—former pastors, old friends, my paternal grandma, my great-grandparents. Then I saw people I somehow knew to be Moses, Abraham, David, Daniel, Ruth, Peter, and Paul. My grandma stood right there in the middle of the circle, looking radiant, her red hair blazing. Then I realized that this was Grandma's welcoming party in heaven. They were greeting her. She was finally home.

The dream had seemed so real, I didn't want to stop thinking about it. But I looked at my clock and realized I had to get ready for church. I hurriedly dressed, grabbed a bite of breakfast, and rushed out the door. I made it in time for choir practice and then sang in the choir. When we finished, as I slipped into the pew behind my mom and dad, Mom turned around and whispered, "We just got a call. Grandma died early this morning."

I suddenly realized that the time of her death was just minutes before I'd awakened that morning. My dream was *true*. Grandma was home in heaven. And, oh, did she have a welcoming party! My heart swelled within me as tears filled my eyes.

We packed up and drove to be with Grandpa in Wichita. The hours were filled with preparations. I was wrapped in the afterglow of my wonderful dream, but I missed Grandma enormously.

After the memorial service the next Tuesday, we decided to go to dinner.

We'd forgotten it was Halloween and were somewhat surprised to see the servers and staff dressed in costumes. Then our waitress came, and I was astonished. She was dressed like an angel, and her halo encircled a flaming mass of red curls!

And then I really understood. Although Grandma was gone, my heavenly Father had promised to send his angels to watch over us. He'd even sent a redheaded angel to our table as a tangible reminder.

—Linn Kane, Bartlesville, Oklahoma

Security With a Sword

After relocating to a new city for a job, I bought a house in a quaint district next to a large park filled with beautiful old trees. I didn't realize the area was teeming with drug traffickers. I'd learned quickly that one dealer lived next door; his "customers" frequented the neighborhood at all hours of the night.

I called an alarm company to price a monitored security system. As I considered the $35-a-month commitment, the thought occurred to me, *Why, for that price I could sponsor a child through Compassion International!*

Suddenly a second, even stronger "thought" landed. I felt God saying, "Mayme, if you sponsor that child, I'll be your security system." I sponsored Stephen Henrique, a beautiful little boy from Colombia, then went about my business living life in my new home and trusting God to be my protection.

My job required long hours and I often got home after dark, too late to walk safely in the park that was a stone's throw away. This had become a popular place for dealers and users, and police had been trying to clean it up, but it was still no place for a woman to be walking alone after hours.

Nevertheless, determined not to live in fear—and remembering that I had *the* top-of-the-line "security system"—I often laced up my tennis shoes and hit the sidewalks that meandered through the tree-lined park.

One night a patrol car pulled up next to me. A policeman lowered the window and asked, "Have you seen any suspicious characters in the area?"

My heart sped up. "No, officer, I haven't seen anyone."

"Let us know if you do," he said. "We've gotten several calls from people reporting a seven-foot-tall man walking around the park, wearing a white muscle shirt and carrying a sword."

No joke!

I assured him I'd call if I saw anyone fitting the description. As his car pulled away, I couldn't help but laugh out loud with delight and gratitude.

I'm sure the officer had just described my guardian angel.

—Mayme Shroyer, Colorado Springs, Colorado

Healed in the Holy Land

A few years ago, my wife, Barbara, and I took a tour of the Holy Land with twenty-four other couples. One day, we went to the Church of the Holy Sepulchre in Jerusalem to have mass in the tomb, believed by many to be the place Jesus' body was laid after the crucifixion. Since the space is small, the members of our group took turns entering to partake in mass, led by a priest.

The couple in front of us in line was from Michigan, and the woman had recently been diagnosed with bowel cancer, though she'd told no one on the trip. (We discovered this later.) She had put off surgery until she returned from Israel. In the tomb was a picture above the table where Christ had been laid. The woman reached over the table and raised the picture, which was on a hinge. She then reached into the space behind the picture and felt a shock, like an electrical charge.

When she walked out of the tomb, she came upon a Franciscan priest sitting by the door. He motioned to her to come close to him so he could tell her something. He blessed her, touched her, and said with a nod of his head, "You may go now."

When her surgeon examined her back in Michigan, he found absolutely no evidence of cancer. She had been cured.

—John Willke, Cincinnati, Ohio

Quick Recovery

Not long ago my wife, Anoosh, began to have severe pain in her jaw. An MRI showed a black mass in her upper jawbone. The doctor was fairly certain it was cancer, but couldn't be 100 percent positive until the day of her operation.

I sat in the waiting room, praying intently. Finally he came out and said that yes, it was cancer, and that they'd excised a portion for a biopsy to confirm. I went to the parking lot for an hour and a half, crying out to God.

The doctor met me at the door when I came back. He said, "We don't understand this, but when we opened your wife's jaw, both the other physician and I saw cancer. We had to remove all her teeth on that side because there was no bone left. It must have been a miracle. We both saw cancer, yet the biopsy came back negative. By the time we sewed her jaw back together there was no sign of cancer."

Anoosh has been cancer-free ever since.

—Alan Bullock, Colleyville, Texas

The Day the Seizures Stopped

When I was considering proposing marriage to my then-girlfriend, Barbara, her father recommended changing my mind because she'd battled life-threatening seizures her entire life. She would need 24/7 care and incur costly medical bills for the rest of her days. Undeterred, we chose to marry and resolved to do the best we could to manage her medical situation.

One day, while home, Barbara had a strong impression—she felt that God had healed her and that she no longer needed to take the medications required to control the seizures. I certainly believed in God's ability to heal, yet I worried for her safety and well-being. I insisted she take the meds during the week and, instead, not take them on the weekends so I could be there in case she began having a seizure.

A few days later I was at work when the Lord told me there was nothing I could do that he couldn't do himself. I rushed home to tell Barbara she could stop taking all medications. That was many years ago, and to date, ever since that time, she has been 100 percent seizure-free.

—Benny Tate, Milner, Georgia

EPILOGUE

What's Your Story?

Miracle stories fascinate our minds, fortify our faith, and fuel our hope.

More than anything, miracles remind us that we're not alone in this often-frightening world. Even when circumstances are at their darkest and we feel like a David preparing to meet our own Goliath, miracle stories bolster our belief that there is a spiritual dimension every bit as real as the physical dimension we can see, hear, touch, and taste. We're reassured that there truly is a plan and purpose for our lives—and, most important, someone helping us to fulfill that unique plan and purpose.

In this book, you've met dozens of people for whom the word *miracle* has taken on intensely personal meaning. In the midst of facing what seemed like insurmountable challenges, illness, or grief, something changed and the unexplainable happened. The tide turned. What was lost was found. Second chances were embraced. Grace was granted.

You've been entertained and perhaps even inspired by these stories about amazing things that happened to others.

But what about *you*?

There's a good chance that, as you look back over the pages of your life, you have your own miraculous story to tell. Perhaps you've never told it in a collection like this one, but it's just as astounding and life-changing as any of these experiences. The sad truth is that while our miracles are real, our memories are fallible and our gratitude can fade over time until, eventually, as we look back, the miraculous evokes little more awe than the mundane.

Or maybe you can't point to a single breathtaking miraculous event. Even if this is the case, there has been a series of decisions, events, and surprises that have helped get you to where you are today. What some people would call coincidence or good fortune you call God's involvement. You've been reassured that God sees you and cares about you.

Miracles happen. They've happened to those in this book, and they've happened to you. One challenge each of us faces is keeping ourselves from allowing the passage of time and the fading of memories to rob us of the wonder we felt when a miracle was new. Another challenge is keeping ourselves from dismissing seemingly "small" miracles and so underestimating not only their impact but also the one who intervened.

Whether or not you're aware of it, the truth is that mysteries do exist, and there absolutely, positively is a plan and purpose for your life.

It's our hope and prayer that these stories will encourage you to turn an enlightened eye on your own life, that they will remind you of the times God has intervened, and that they will put "lucky coincidences" in a new light too.

It's also our desire that these stories enlarge your hope and expand your faith. Trusting that God can intervene—and walking day by day anticipating his loving touch—is the best way to live. In fact, it opens the door for him to move freely in your life. *All* blessings find their source in him: "Every good and perfect gift is from above, coming down from the Father of the heavenly lights, who does not change like shifting shadows" (James 1:17).

Look for those gifts. In your past. In your present. In your future. Your story is every bit as wonderful and God-directed as the stories in this book.

ACKNOWLEDGMENTS

From Jim Garlow:

Every book is a collaborative effort involving not merely an author (or authors) but also a large team of editors, marketers, publishers, people running printing presses, people driving forklifts in warehouses, and trucks carrying completed books down freeways, along with many others. This book, no exception, involved a large team effort.

I've coauthored numerous books, the last four with Keith Wall. In most shared situations, I've written approximately half the book. In some cases, my coauthor and I divided up chapters. In other cases (as with our previous "Garlow and Wall" books), my coauthor wrote each chapter's story portion and I wrote its teaching segment.

On this book, though, my task was to find creative ways to locate the stories, then procure them by casting the net widely, and then doing only the first stage of vetting.

My coauthor had the heavy lifting: the next two stages of interviewing and the writing. Then my task was to review the writing, and, finally, to handle all interviews and media as the book was released.

Simply stated, I've never done so little actual personal writing on a book. To Keith Wall goes this credit. I want to acknowledge my wonderful and skillful "co-laborer" for the massive load he bore in this exciting project.

In addition, special mention—well-deserved and hard-earned—goes to Pam Dahl, who managed myriad details, always with good humor and a cheerful attitude. Thank you, Pam.

From Keith Wall:

It's said that the most important part of any journey is who you travel with—and I am exceedingly blessed in life with some fabulous traveling companions. Everyone should be so fortunate to walk arm in arm with people like . . .

Alan Wartes, whose extraordinary creative talent and integrity never fail to inspire me. His assistance with this book was invaluable.

Kyle Duncan, who pours out grace and compassion by the bucketful.

Dave Kopp, whose off-kilter take on life almost always proves to be on-kilter.

Karen Linamen, whose bright spirit and upbeat attitude chase away shadows and usher in light.

Dave Reitz, a loyal, faithful friend if ever there was one.

My coauthor, Jim Garlow, has endured extraordinary challenges and hardships for as long as I've known him—with unwavering faith and without a word of complaint. He has my utmost respect and admiration.

Our editor, Christopher Soderstrom, epitomizes the word *unflappable*, despite the many reasons we've given him to be "flapped." Since editors are often the unsung heroes of the publishing biz, I am happy to sing his praises.

I want to express my sincere gratitude to Nancy Renich, copy editor, who diligently and dependably serves authors (including this one), often without our knowing it. And to Alex Fane, file manager, who heroically and humbly saves the day when problems arise (which, in this trade, is quite regularly). Sincere thanks also to LaVonne Downing, manager of Bethany House's production department, who competently handles a thousand behind-the-scenes details and duties.

As always, I deeply appreciate the encouragement and support of my family, Robin, Juliana, and Logan. My cup runneth over.

JAMES L. GARLOW (PhD, Drew University) is senior pastor of Skyline Church in San Diego, chairman of Renewing American Leadership, a nationwide speaker, and author. He has appeared on CNN, FOX, NBC, and other media outlets. *The Garlow Perspective* commentary is heard on over 800 radio outlets. Jim and his family live in San Diego, California. Learn more at www.jimgarlow.com.

KEITH WALL, a twenty-five-year publishing veteran, has been an award-winning magazine editor, radio scriptwriter, and online columnist. He currently writes full time in collaboration with numerous bestselling authors. He and his family live in Colorado.

Get to know Dr. Jim Garlow...

www.JimGarlow.com (Personal)

www.SkylineChurch.org (Pastoral)

www.ToRenewAmerica.com (National)

Connect on Facebook

Hear Dr. Jim Garlow on his radio commentary
The Garlow Perspective.

(For station listings, go to www.AmbassadorAdvertising.com)

More True Stories and Spiritual Wisdom From James L. Garlow and Keith Wall

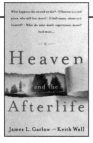

A bestselling author and a respected pastor offer a straightforward biblical take on heaven, hell, and things encountered "on the other side."

Heaven and the Afterlife

A fascinating compilation of real-life afterlife encounters. Writing from a biblical perspective, the authors offer a message of comfort, hope, and inspiration—and a reminder that there is more to life than what we can see in the here and now.

Encountering Heaven and the Afterlife

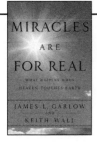

Bestselling authors share evidence of God at work in our world; carefully examine biblical teaching about miracles; and provide honest, trustworthy information that will boost your faith.

Miracles Are for Real

◊ BETHANYHOUSE